Classical Antiquity

A Captivating Guide to Ancient Greece and Rome and How These Civilizations Influenced Europe, North Africa, and Western Asia

Free Bonus from Captivating History (Available for a Limited time)

Hi History Lovers!

Now you have a chance to join our exclusive history list so you can get your first history ebook for free as well as discounts and a potential to get more history books for free! Simply visit the link below to join.

Captivatinghistory.com/ebook

Also, make sure to follow us on Facebook, Twitter and Youtube by searching for Captivating History.

Contents

Introduction

The story of Athens, Rome, Hellas, and the Roman Republic begins with a warm, blue sea upon whose waters a handful of humble canoes drift from shore to shore. Farmers populated the high hills of the pre-Hellenic realm, sowing barley and wheat, and reaping olives and grapes for making oil and wine. Families grew enough food to feed themselves, with perhaps a little left over to sell at the local community market.

Soon, Minoan and Phoenician traders learned to construct great wooden galley boats capable of delivering a group of people safely from one city or town to another by means of dozens of oars. In good winds, the mariners could drop the boat's sails and rest their arms while the breeze did the work. An assortment of Greeks, Italians, Carthaginians, Egyptians, Persians, and Etruscans learned how to row and sail these waters in search of grains, vegetables, fruit, textiles, pottery, weapons, and precious metals. Curiosity and migration patterns made these people neighbors, but necessity made them trading partners and allies—and eventually rivals.

From about the 9th to 5th centuries BCE, the population of Greece grew unprecedently large, expanding from about 800,000 people to as many as 13 million.[1] About a quarter million of these lived in Athens.[2] The average size of urban households during this period grew considerably, a fact that suggests that food was suddenly available in excesses sufficient to keep larger families healthy and alive much more effectively than just a millennium earlier.[3] Bigger families meant bigger armies and larger communities that would eventually grow into the metropolises of Classical Greece.

This incredible stretch of time is called Classical Antiquity; the age in which Western civilization first realized its potential and place in the world. The era brought on big changes for all the people of the Mediterranean. Thanks to new agricultural methods, seafaring technology, and trade, great civilizations sprang up around the sea, building large urban centers full of artists, merchants, political thinkers, scientists, and philosophers. As Greco-Roman culture grew, the relationships each city and realm had with one another also developed and changed.

It began in Greece.

[1] Sealey, Raphael. *A History of the Greek City States.* 1976.
[2] Thorley, J. *Athenian Democracy.* 2005
[3] Ault, Bradley, A. "Oikos and Oikonomia: Greek Houses, Households and the Domestic Economy." 2007.

Chapter 1 – A Blind Poet from Ionia

Pre-Athenian Greece was not yet the shining beacon of culture and intellect that it would become, but even centuries before the greatest philosophers of that glistening city-state emerged, Greece was a country of love and art. A blind poet of that era, well-educated for his day, and deeply talented, was lucky to have found himself in such a society that treasured his gifts of oratory and song. Other civilizations may have left him to struggle terribly, but not that of the ancient Ionians. Theirs was a well-populated region on the northeastern coast of the Mediterranean Sea, which was part of the western Greek settlement. There, according to the ancient Greek historian Herodotus,[4] a bard and historian called Homer was given quarter. [5] His poems were received with joy and his tales remembered for endless generations. These are the first stories and myths the world knows of that ancient people before their country

---

[4] Herodotus, *Histories.* Written in 440 BCE, Herodotus notes in this manuscript that he believes Homer lived 400 years before him.

[5] Though the full authorship of the *Odyssey* and the *Iliad* is ascribed to Homer, most researchers agree that the works were added to regularly over the centuries by successive storytellers and historians who came after him. Source: Kahane, Ahuvia. *Homer: A Guide for the Perplexed.* 2012.

blossomed into a legend of its own: the first full bloom of Western civilization.

During Homer's time, a new alphabet was being used to replace the lost writing system of the Mycenaeans.[6] Based on that of the Phoenicians, the Greek alphabet featured 24 letters meant to represent both consonants and vowel sounds. The alphabet followed Greek sailors to exotic destinations and took on new forms and slight variations in many port cities of the Mediterranean Sea. In Ionia, Homer's use of Greek in his popular epic poems helped the language catch on in surrounding realms, much as the printing press would do in the European Middle Ages.

It was probably sometime in the late 8th century BCE when Homer composed his most epic works: two long-form poems in ancient Greek that chronicled the ten-year Trojan War—a pillar of Greek mythology—and the long journey home of the lost hero, Odysseus.[7] The Trojan War is in itself a milestone of European history— whether or not it truly did occur. Archaeologists, like C. Brian Rose, professor of classical archaeology at the University of Pennsylvania, believe that Troy was a city in ancient Turkey whose geographical location was strategically necessary for migration and trade to the Near East. Rose surmises that there were many wars fought between the Greeks and Anatolians throughout Classical Antiquity, of which Homer's story is one.[8]

It may be that Homer's writings were largely fictional works, but they marked an important milestone in the journey of human evolution; for the first time in the Western world, literature, intellect, and art were prized and rewarded enough that an individual could pursue them singularly. Homer, though perhaps not technically an

---

[6] Herodotus. Ibid.

[7] Altschuler, E., Calude, A., Meade, A., and Pagel, Mark. "Linguistic Evidence Supports Date for Homeric Epics." 2013.

[8] Rose, C. Brian. "Assessing the Evidence for the Trojan Wars." 2004.

author or writer, is still considered the very first literary mind of the Western world. Though he probably never pressed stylus to waxed tablet, Homer did compose epic poems in memory of the legendary Trojan War. It was and still is an event so ancient and shrouded in mystery that it is at once considered myth and ancient history.

In his two lengthy installments, the *Iliad* and the *Odyssey*, Homer tells the story of the siege of the city of Troy by an alliance of Greek tribes. The first story was set during the last year of the war, and through a plot that centers on King Agamemnon and the warrior Achilles, the finer details of that siege are laid out. The *Odyssey* then follows the long voyage of one of the heroes of that long war, Odysseus, as he travels home to Ithaca. Both stories use a multitude of deities as both major and minor characters, including Aphrodite, Athena, and Apollo, who literally enter the battlefield on both sides of the clash between the Trojans and Greeks.

Close to 3,000 years later, most Western civilizations still know at least part of the legendary story of the Trojan War. It begins with the kidnapping of the beautiful Queen Helen from King Menelaus of Sparta, and it ends with the false gift of a giant, wooden horse. Indeed, the stories of the blind Ionian poet are not just examples of ancient literature; they are proof of humanity's creativity and endless love of tales of adventure with surprise endings.

Ancient as they may be, Homer's words are stunningly beautiful and full of feeling. Far from a dry retelling of facts and events, Homer's poems were crafted to entice his listeners into emotionally connecting with the events of the past. He was sure to entangle the hearts of audiences into the stories with clever usage of contemporary cultural norms, like dialogue between multiple Greek gods:

> Men are so quick to blame the gods: they say
>
> that we devise their misery. But they
>
> themselves- in their depravity- design

grief greater than the griefs that fate assigns.

Of course, since Homer likely never did write anything down—and perhaps never knew how to write at all—his stories were remembered through the act of being told again and again. This was the way of Homer and his ancestors who were adept at recollecting what equated to thousands of pages of words, lines, stanzas, and paragraphs. For Homer, it was probably made easier thanks to his use of the lyre, which was a staple instrument for all the storytellers in his poems. Put to music, poetry was doubly entertaining and much easier to commit to memory.

After all, Homer would not have considered himself a writer but a bard. It was his life's work to tell stories in the form of songs. Legends of Homer, told through the writing of Greek poets and writers who came centuries later, say that he earned his living wandering from town to town, offering to entertain households with his stories.[9] Once he'd been invited in, probably for a dinner party, he would take a chair either at the table or just off to one side, pluck the strings of his lyre, and begin to sing the words he'd pieced together in his mind.

At 176,000 words, the *Iliad* was not a story that could be told in the space of one short evening. As was the custom of bards like Homer, he probably stayed several days with his host family, revealing the tragedy of the Trojan War piece by piece, song by song, until finally reaching the end one final night.

Any moment might be our last. Everything is more beautiful because we're doomed. You will never be lovelier than you are now. We will never be here again.

Human history is plagued with violence, war, battles for dominion and supremacy, and organized by laundry lists of great warriors and emperors. For thousands and thousands of years, those inspired to paint pictures, construct great artworks, propose philosophies, and

---

[9] Scodel, Ruth. "Bardic Performance and Oral Tradition in Homer." 1998.

tell stories were required to otherwise engage their energies into necessities like farming, gardening, herding, grinding grain, and maintaining their homes. Archaeology of the prehistoric world is focused on food, clothing, pottery, and migration; little to nothing exists that belies any celebrated artisans with the exception of great architects. Three millennia ago, however, something amazing happened in Greece. A scattering of urban centers became strong and resourceful enough to support a new type of citizen: the philosopher.

Chapter 2 – Pythagoras

As long as Man continues to be the ruthless destroyer of lower living beings, he will never know health or peace. For as long as men massacre animals, they will kill each other. Indeed, he who sows the seed of murder and pain cannot reap joy and love.

(Pythagoras, as quoted by Ovid in the *Metamorphoses*)

Like Homer, the ancient Ionian Pythagoras did not set out to live his life as common men did. He, too, was fortunate enough to find himself part of a culture in which it was not necessary for him to spend his life farming or herding sheep. Instead, Pythagoras wanted to spend his time understanding the mysteries of the universe.

The man in question was born on Samos, a Mediterranean island that was part of the Ionian League.[10] The son of a Phoenician jeweler from Tyre and a local Greek mother from Samos, young Pythagoras was evidently a popular boy who was eager to learn everything he could about mathematics and religion. Thanks to his aristocratic family, he was able to study at the feet of some of Samos' most respected tutors. Since education had yet to become formalized in 6th-century Greece, students' curriculums could be quite diverse. Generally speaking, male children from reasonably wealthy families would learn the alphabet, numbers, and some basic mathematics. Poorer boys did not receive any such teachings, as they were only

---

[10] Kahn, Charles H. *Pythagoras and the Pythagoreans: A Brief History*. 2001.

able to focus on pertinent tasks related to farming, pastoralism, and home maintenance. Girls were mostly left out of tutoring altogether.

For Pythagoras, learning was everything. He loved mathematics and philosophy, believing that at some ultimate level the two were one and the same. The universe, to him, was made of numbers and equations, and he was compelled to try to combine pieces of each of his subjects into one, all-encompassing philosophy to explain life and the physical world. He believed that if he could extract the most solid theories of philosophy and religion and somehow relate them to the fundamental principles of mathematics, he could achieve this lofty goal.

Pythagoras was inspired by the old Orphic religion which had already fallen out of fashion with the Greeks. Orphics believed that a person had an immortal soul that had been imprisoned in a physical body as punishment for some past sin. The cult of Orpheus was based on the poetry ascribed to the mythical man of the same name who was said to have gone into the depths of the underworld and then returned safely to the surface. Followers believed that if they spent their lives avoiding wrongdoing, their souls would ultimately be released from the prison of the body.

To traditional Orphics, any act from which a person could derive pleasure was sinful and therefore inappropriate. To gain the freedom of one's soul, that person had to subscribe wholeheartedly to asceticism and therefore reject material gains, overindulgence, alcohol, and many activities that the average citizen takes for granted—including sex.[11] As a devoted member of the faith he hoped to reestablish, Pythagoras adopted a meatless diet.

In searching for a unifying theory between his subjects of study, Pythagoras focused his energies away from temptation and—he hoped—entreated the powers that be to look upon him favorably. In his ruminations, he concluded that the divine soul of a person did not

---

[11] Scott, Charles E. *Living with Indifference.* 2007.

perish after death but was usually passed into a new baby. His ideas were ridiculed by most of his peers who offered him little in the way of stimulating conversation since the educational system of his day was rather limited. In search of more knowledge, Pythagoras left his homeland and traveled throughout Greece and the Near East, finally crossing the sea to Egypt.

The Egyptian Kingdom had already reached its impressive zenith and was shrinking in influence and prosperity by Pythagoras' lifetime, but the cities of the still impressive kingdom held a great deal of mystery for the Greek traveler. He went to the great city of Memphis to study with the learned priests and sages there.[12] They taught him new methods in mathematics, as well as imparting their spiritual beliefs onto him as a willing student. The priests revered secrecy in their practice and forbade wearing animal skins while inside the temples. They also forbade eating broad beans,[13] which were not usually grown in any part of Egypt, although they were used as offerings to the gods. The deep sense of commitment and truth that Pythagoras felt in Egypt affected him for the rest of his life, although he did not agree with every rule the priests taught him.

However, the hierarchical system in which Egypt's wise men were revered irritated Pythagoras, whose ascetic mindset moved him to view himself more as a seeker of truth than a holy man. The word he invented to describe himself came from two Greek words: philos and sophia. These meant "lover" and "wisdom," which made a man like Pythagoras a "philos-sophia," or philosopher.[14] As such, he sought to bring balance to the distribution of education, thereby changing the elitist system in place. To this end, he began to take on students and teach them what he'd learned.

---

[12] Joost-Gaugier, Christiane L. *Measuring Heaven: Pythagoras and His Influence on Thought and Art in Antiquity and the Middle Ages.* *2006.*

[13] Lippi, D. "The Broad Bean's Syndrome in Ancient Egypt." 1989.

[14] Guthrie, W. K. C. *A History of Greek Philosophy: Volume 1, The Earlier Presocratics and the Pythagoreans.* 1978.

The inspired teacher found very eager students within the kingdom of the pharaohs, but the happiness he'd discovered there did not last forever. In 525 BCE, the Persian army came to Egypt and forced its way into the heart of the kingdom, ending the nearly 2600-year rule of the renowned Kings of Egypt.[15] More kings were allowed to use that title, but the true power behind the crown was henceforth wielded by King Cambyses II of Persia and his successors. The conquerors took Pythagoras as their prisoner.

He found himself jailed in Babylon, the center of the Middle Eastern civilization of Mesopotamia, for several years. During this time, he dreamed of returning home to Samos and building a new community of teachers, students, and philosophers. When he finally got the chance to do so, however, he found that the island of his birth had changed terribly. Due to political corruption and the tyrannical rule of Polycrates, the roads and buildings had degraded, and the people had grown coarser.[16]

Pythagoras founded his school despite these changes and became a national icon. His academy, named the Semicircle, closely followed the curricula of Egyptian schools he'd frequented during his time abroad.[17] He worked hard to cultivate the community of intellects he had hoped to bring together, but ultimately, his efforts were in vain. This was not the right place in which to recruit intelligent, enthusiastic people for his new community.

So, Pythagoras left Samos once more and took to the sea, this time to the west. He landed at the Greek colony of Croton, on the modern Italian mainland, and established a new community. It was here, in the wandering philosopher's final home, that he brought together the keen seekers of knowledge whose company he had craved all his

---

[15] Bunson, Margaret. *Encylopedia of Ancient Egypt*. 2014.

[16] Shipley, Graham. *A History of Samos, 800-188 BC*. 1987.

[17] Karamanides, Dimitra. *Pythagoras: Pioneering Mathematician and Musical Theorist of Ancient Greece*. 2005.

life.[18] Males and females both came to Pythagoras for lessons, and he taught them indiscriminately, instructing them in his ways of unified sciences and Orphic beliefs. Most of the students probably followed in their teacher's footsteps, rejecting meat and dedicating their actions to the betterment of their divine souls.

Pythagoras' name has become synonymous with the development of the self-named Pythagorean theorem, which is a cornerstone of advanced geometry. In mathematics, a theorem is equal to a law, except that it has been proven on the basis of several other laws. Pythagoras' theorem relates to right triangles, stating that the square of the hypotenuse (the side of the triangle opposite from the right angle) is equal to the sum of the squares of the other two sides. It is written as $a^2+b^2=c^2$.

This equation allows anyone to determine the length of any side of a right triangle as long as the other two lengths are already known. Ironically, though Pythagoras is often credited with the discovery of this relationship between the sides of a right triangle, this particular geometric law was already known in Babylon and Egypt. Pythagoras could have learned it during his time with the monks in Babylon or with the priests of Memphis and simply introduced it to the Greeks for the first time upon his return.[19]

Right triangles were not his only mathematical pursuit. Pythagoras also challenged the idea that the Earth was flat, a concept that remained in fashion despite his astronomical research. His study of the shadows of the Earth falling across the moon during lunar eclipses helped him conclude that the Earth was indeed a sphere. Otherwise, he posited, how could the Earth consistently cast shadows with curved edges?[20]

---

[18] Ibid.

[19] Ratner, Bruce. "Pythagoras: Everyone knows his famous theorem, but not who discovered it 1000 years before him." 2009.

[20] Couper, Heather and Henbest, Nigel. *The Story of Astronomy: How the Universe Revealed Its Secrets.*

A spiritual man dedicated to the pursuit and study of music, Pythagoras insisted that music was just as much a part of the universe as were the tides and the seasons. Naturally, he worked musical theory into his mathematical pursuits, believing that the relationship between notes and the length of the strings on a lyre could be represented by a mathematical ratio. He also believed that the planets of the solar system each produced a specific note.[21] In his mind, the universe was made of music that he would never be able to hear.

Pythagoras died in mysterious circumstances, and his school was burned to the ground by political enemies.[22] Historians are unsure if he ever married or had children. Nevertheless, his teachings and way of life persisted in Greece and the Mediterranean for centuries after he passed away. His discoveries and lifestyle greatly influenced the philosophers that were yet to come and further shape our understanding of the world and humanity's place in it.

---

[21] Ibid.

[22] Kahn, Charles H. *Pythagoras and the Pythagoreans.* 2001.

Chapter 3 – Athens, Greece

Greece was originally home to four ancient tribes (Ionians, Achaeans, Aeolians, and Dorians) from which many branches of Greek civilization were derived. While Homer and his nameless successors performed in the households of Ionia and Pythagoras wandered the known world looking for answers to life's most complex questions, the Greeks upon the mainland retained a semi-nomadic lifestyle. Families and small, tightly-knit communities of Greeks spent centuries roaming the land and temporarily staying in the towns they founded before moving on. In Athens, many of them eventually found a permanent home.[23]

It was here that a group of ancient farmers inhabited the lands of the high hills where they could grow barley, wheat, pomegranates, figs, grapes, and olives. Perched among the low mountaintops and not too far from the shore of the Mediterranean Sea, these farmers flourished as many as 3,000 years before that spot became a metropolis.[24] First only a small village, hardly the most impressive in the Greek lands,

---

[23] Sacks, David; Murray, Oswyn; and Brody, Lisa R. *Encylopedia of the Ancient Greek World.* 2014.

[24] Immerwahr, S. *The Athenian Agora XII: The Neolithic and Bronze Age.* 1971.

Athens persisted, slowly attracting settlers away from the nomadic traditions of the wilds. By the 5th century BCE, Athens was a beautiful city built with hewn stone and filled with religious buildings and objects that served the people's overwhelming need to worship the many deities of their ancestors.[25] Much of its success was due to its proximity to the sea.

Nearby, just over 11 kilometers (7 miles) southwest of the budding city, was the busy port city of Piraeus. Humans lived there for at least 2,000 years before Athens was settled; they fished, farmed, and collected salt along the low-lying flats that connected their settlement with the mainland.[26] Athenians would make the trip to gather salt when the flats were dry and exposed, though for much of the year, the port village was physically cut off from them by the risen sea.[27] These were the glory days for Athens when trade between North Africa, Europe, and western Asia was busy and exciting. The markets at Piraeus overflowed with olives, oil, wine, Italian wood, Egyptian grains, honey, silver, pottery, fish, eels, mutton, goat, animal hides, shellfish, and even slaves. Thanks to this once humble port, Athens and other cities along the Mediterranean Sea expanded rapidly, establishing one of the most important and influential cultural networks in the ancient world.

For Athens, communications with the outside world were crucial to its own growth and perseverance, particularly since only about one-fifth of Greece's total landmass was suitable for cultivation.[28] Though they did grow their own grains, the barley, wheat, and millet crops were very dependent on ideal weather conditions, and from year to year, their yields fluctuated greatly. In smaller quantities, the early Athenians grew broad beans, chickpeas, and lentils. Other

---

[25] Kleiner, Fred S. *Gardner's Art Through the Ages: A Global History.* 2009.

[26] Protopapas, Athanassios. *Proceedings of the European Cognitive Science Conference.* 2007.

[27] **Apostolopoulos**,G; Goiran, Jean-Philippe; **Pavlopoulos**, Kosmas; and Fouache, Eric. "Was the Piraeus peninsula (Greece) a rocky island?" 2014.

[28] Harlan Hale, William. *Horizon History of Ancient Greece.* 2017.

sources of food included cucumbers, apples, pears, pomegranates, onions, garlic, almonds, and walnuts. These were nutritious, but the Athenians needed more grain to sustain a larger population. At Piraeus, they imported exactly what they needed from nearby traders in search of fruit, oil, and fish.

With their food sources established, Athens proper and its surrounding region—called Attica—swelled to a population of about 300,000 in the 5th century BCE.[29] An estimated 50,000 of those people were slaves, and about 30,000 of them were adult males with the right to participate in political elections.[30] Despite the sharp lines that were drawn between voters and non-voters, this is the first well-documented example of a well-organized democracy in the world and certainly the first of its kind in Western civilization. It was here that the first principles of government by the people were discussed in their finest details.

Before Athenian democracy overtook the rule of the aristocratic archons, however, the people needed the help of its educated, influential reformist citizens. One of the first to condemn the city's oligarchic political model was Solon, born in Attica around 636 BCE.[31] Ironically, Solon was born into a noble family who could trace its lineage back to Codrus, one of the last demi-gods who ruled as King of Athens. Though his family was not particularly wealthy, it was very influential, and in his youth, Solon found himself at the head of an Athenian army whose purpose was to possess the island of Salamis. Salamis lies just a few miles offshore from Piraeus, making it a strategic location for port and merchant developments.

[29] De Ligt, Luuk, and Laurens E. Tacoma (editors.) *Migration and Mobility in the Early Roman Empire*. 1967.

[30] **Rothchild, John. *Introduction to Athenian Democracy of the Fifth and Fourth Centuries BCE*.** 2007.

[31] Stanton, G. R. *Athenian Politics c. 800–500 BC: A Sourcebook*. 1990.

A faction of Attica fought against this usurpation, but eventually, the island was granted to Athens by a neutral Spartan envoy who was asked to intervene.[32] Afterward, Solon was made an archon of Athens and the realm, granting him political powers over the entire city and its greater urban area. Eight other men had the same position, and these nine leaders were meant to administer the various facets of Athens based on forthright discussion and agreement amongst themselves.

Solon had grand ideas for the people of Athens, but he knew that those ideas would be harshly questioned by the other eight archons. Solon considered himself a man of equality, but the position of archon was held by members of Athens' wealthiest families whom he knew firsthand would reject reform that favored the city's poor. Daringly, Solon made several unprecedented rulings without the counsel of his fellow archons and immediately fled the city to avoid the repercussions.

The most controversial new ruling was to erase all public debts. Solon was not only held accountable for this reform in itself but for the fact that his own friends and family had known about it beforehand. Having taken out loans prior to the reforms, these friends knew perfectly well that they would not have to make any repayments. Solon had also legislated that more men of Athens could enter the Assembly, the central governing body of the city in which citizens discussed and voted on issues of the day.[33] It was a means to take the power of government out of the hands of just the aristocrats and share the ownership of the city with its middle class. Having redefined "citizenship" to include any male land-owning person within Attica, Solon's law allowed 400 representative citizens to meet together and administrate the daily laws and issues of the city-state. This assembly was called the boule, and its

---

[32] Plutarch. *Plutarch's Lives.*

[33] E. Harris, *A New Solution to the Riddle of the Seisachtheia*, in *The Development of the Polis in Archaic Greece*. 1997.

members were elected by a much larger body of all the realm's adult male citizens.[34]

Sadly, Solon was not able to enjoy the wonderful gifts he'd given the middle-class Athenians since he had left Greece altogether and embarked on a ten-year journey that took him all around the Mediterranean. Much like the voyages and adventures of Homer's Odysseus, Solon's travels took him over thousands of miles of ocean and land to meet foreign dignitaries like Pharaoh Amasis II of Egypt.[35] It was the sort of life befitting a poet, which is exactly what Solon preferred to be. Some of his works are included in *Plutarch's Lives*:

> Some wicked men are rich, some good are poor;
>
> We will not change our virtue for their store:
>
> Virtue's a thing that none can take away,
>
> But money changes owners all the day.

Solon's reforms would not last the century, but their premise and ideals far outlasted the man himself. Cleisthenes took up the reins of fair government and democracy once more in 507 BCE, judging that every free man over the age of eighteen living in Attica was a citizen of Athens with the right to representation in the Assembly.[36] Still, only land-owning citizens could serve as those representatives, but it was a fairer system than it had been. This legislation held firm until the Archon Ephialtes convinced his fellow high rulers of the city to further minimize the power of the nobility, granting them only the authority to rule over court cases of murder or sacrilege.[37] This came

---

[34] McGlew, James F. *Tyranny and Political Culture in Ancient Greece.* 2018.

[35] Moyer, Ian S. *Egypt and the Limits of Hellenism.* 2011.

[36] Ackermann, M, et al (editors.) *Encyclopedia of World History: Volume I.* 2008.

[37] Thorley, J. *Athenian Democracy.* 2005.

to pass in 462 BCE when democracy in Athens was firmly established.[38]

---

[38] Tangian, Andranik. *Mathematical Theory of Democracy.* 2013.

Chapter 4 – The Greek Pantheon

The stories of the gods of Greece are much older than any of the cities of Classical Antiquity—even those of Ionia. Tablets containing their names even predate the form of Greek writing used by Homer.[39] At least a dozen gods and goddesses, each with his or her own set of powers and characteristics, ruled ancient Hellas for thousands of years before the old ways broke apart and the age of Christianity began. In fact, these beliefs were probably so strong and enduring because they were reinforced across the known world of the Greeks, including the cultures of the Norse, the Italians, and even the Indus River Valley civilization.

Ancient migration and trade patterns almost certainly spread the stories of hundreds of different gods and goddesses from one end of Europe to another, stretching across western Asia and down into India. The creation story of the Greeks is one that still resonates with people of the Mediterranean. It begins with Chaos.[40]

---

[39] Sacks, D, et al. *Encyclopedia of the Ancient Greek World.* 2014.

[40] David Leeming and Margaret Leeming, A DICTIONARY OF CREATION MYTHS.1994.

Chaos was black nothingness, empty and void and without purpose. From its void, the Earth Mother, Gaia, sprang forth. She was the physical form of the Earth, a deity in itself that would come to nurture all the people and creatures of the world. She was not the only form that appeared out of Chaos, either. Next, there was Eros, Tartarus (the Abyss), and Erebus, the gods of love, the underworld, and the deep darkness. As they all dwelt together in Chaos, Gaia became pregnant without taking a male counterpart and gave birth to Uranus, the sky god, as well as his brother Pontus, god of the ocean.

Gaia and Uranus became lovers, and from their union, the twelve Titans were born. Their union also bore the Cyclopes and the Hecatoncheires. Though the Titans resembled giant humans, the Cyclopes had only one eye, and the three Hecatoncheires had a hundred hands and fifty heads each. Uranus was horrified with his offspring and decided to hide them away deep within Tartarus, the abyss inside Gaia, in exile. The first gods were not only sentient and powerful beings but the physical spaces that were the earth, sky, underworld, and greater universe. So, Uranus was able to lock his horrifying children up within the underworld of the earth that was also his wife.

Gaia did not want to hide her children away, and she called down to them, advising them to rise up against their father and take their place among the gods. Only one of her children answered her plea: The Titan Cronus. Cronus fought his father and castrated him, throwing the god's genitals into the sea. He then took his place at the head of the gods and invited his Titan brothers and sisters to attend him as their king. Cronus married his sister Rhea, who became known as the goddess of motherhood and fertility. Soon, however, Cronus sent the Cyclopes and the Hecatoncheires back into Tartarus, betraying and angering his mother. Despite his treachery, Cronus ruled over the universe for thousands of years in which multitudes of gods and creatures were born, including a line of humans who never aged.

Cronus was told by his parents that he was destined to be overthrown by one of his own children since that was how he'd gained his own power. To avoid such disgrace, Cronus ate the children Rhea birthed, swallowing them whole. Five children were disposed of in this way until Rhea tricked her husband into eating a stone wrapped in a swaddling cloth instead of their sixth child, Zeus. Zeus was then secreted into a cave in Crete where he could grow to adulthood in safety. The baby matured well but came to hate his father, and he vowed to overthrow the Titan ruler. With the help of his wife, the Titan goddess of wisdom, Metis, Zeus fed Cronus a potion that caused him to purge all of his swallowed children. The plan worked, and out came all of Zeus' siblings: Hera, Hades, Poseidon, Demeter, and Hestia. In addition to Cronus' children came the stone wrapped in a blanket.

Next, Zeus traveled to Tartarus and freed the Cyclopes and the Hecatoncheires. Together, the aunts, uncles, and siblings of Zeus hid themselves away in Mount Olympus to plan the overthrow of the cannibalistic ruler of the universe. While they remained hidden, the freed creatures showered gifts upon Zeus and his siblings in thanks for their freedom. For Zeus, they crafted a magical thunderbolt that he could throw at his enemies. For Hades, they fashioned a helmet of invisibility. Poseidon received a trident that could shake the earth. With these powerful tools, they sprang upon Cronus and began the ten-year war that would be known as the Titanomachy.

The Titans whom Cronus had spared from the abyss fought on his side against the Olympians, but Prometheus and Themis defended Zeus. In the end, Zeus was victorious, and all the Titans except those who fought with him were sent back to Tartarus. The Hecatoncheires were stationed at its gates to ensure no one escaped. The Titan Atlas, for leading Cronus' army against the Olympians, was sentenced to hold up the sky for eternity.

As for the valiant Olympians, Zeus had his siblings and himself draw lots. Zeus drew the sky that burdened Atlas. Hades was granted the underworld, Poseidon gained dominion over the oceans and seas of the earth, Demeter was granted agriculture, and Hestia the home and hearth. As for Hera, Zeus tricked her into marrying him, and therefore she became the goddess of marriage and birth. Theirs was an unhappy marriage fraught with rebellion and treachery, as had been Zeus' first marriage. He had swallowed his first bride, Metis, when she became pregnant with their daughter Athena.

Zeus and his growing family ruled from Mount Olympus and oversaw the world of men, whose lives were forever changed from the long war of the gods. Now, the humans lived short lives full of trials and tribulations, aging and weakening as the years moved on. Still, they were a favorite race of the Olympians, and Zeus himself created the Macedonian race, which was an integral piece of the Greek civilization located on the northern end of the Greek mainland.

The mythology of the Greeks was just as influential as the ancient people themselves; in fact, early Romans took the Greeks' creation story and nearly copied it word for word and god for god. The two are almost indistinguishable from one another, and together, they form the spiritual backdrop of the Greco-Roman civilizations of Classical Antiquity.

Chapter 5 – The Expulsion of the Persians

In the 5th century BCE, the Persian Empire was the most powerful in Europe and the Near East. Its borders stretched from Macedon to Egypt to India, and its powerful King Darius the Great wanted to stretch his domain even farther, south from Macedon and Thrace all the way to the Aegean Sea.[41] Athens, Corinth, and Sparta were in direct danger of losing everything to the powerful Persian army. When the Persian army landed at Marathon, 26 miles from the city of Athens, in 490 BCE, the Greeks were quite outnumbered—but they were not without experience in warfare.[42]

The poorest of the Athenians had nothing to fight with except for sticks and spears, but that was not the case for Athens' wealthy men. During the Bronze Age, their armor was hammered from bronze into breastplates, helmets, and sometimes shield coverings, and it was used by soldiers called hoplites.[43] Athens had thousands of hoplites at the disposal of the archons, and by the time Persia invaded, the

---

[41] Briant, Pierre. *From Cyrus to Alexander: A History of the Persian Empire.* 2002.

[42] Tucker, Spencer C. (editor.) *A Global Chronology of Conflict.* 2009.

[43] Kagan, Donald and Gregory F. Viggiano (editors.) *Men of Bronze: Hoplite Warfare in Ancient Greece.* 2013.

uniform of the hoplites had evolved into a full suit of armor. The suit was comprised of bronze defense plates that covered a warrior's upper body, head, and legs. Soldiers were armed with an iron sword and a lance and always carried a large shield. Hoplite warfare was new to the landscape in that it was the first time in Greek history that soldiers were employed solely to don their armor, spear, and shield and remain at the ready for battle.

Hoplites normally were employed to keep Athens safe from its own neighbors—especially Sparta—but this time they had to fight an unfamiliar foe. Together, the men of Athens readied themselves for battle against an indomitable enemy. They were outnumbered two to one. In desperate need of help, Athens sent its best runner, Pheidippides, to Sparta to beg for their assistance. He ran 250 kilometers (155 miles) in two days to reach Sparta, but the warriors of that city were obliged to forego warfare during a religious festival that was taking place.[44] Pheidippides despaired, but there was nothing more to be done. Several days later, the Spartan army marched north to aid its neighbor and found that Athens' soldiers had achieved victory all on their own. 6,000 Persians had been killed in the course of a day, and the city still stood, independent under the power of the archons.[45]

A general in the army, Themistocles, was deeply affected by the attack. He felt that one victory against the Persians was not sufficient to consider Athens safe. A powerful man in Athens who was raised up to the heights of political greatness in the democratic system, Themistocles had the ear of city leaders when he insisted on revamping Athens' military arsenal. Since Athens' gateway was the Aegean Sea, Themistocles suggested heavy investments in new galleys.[46] He wanted to protect his city with a fleet of triremes, boats

---

[44] Karnazes, Dean. *The Road to Sparta.* 2016.

[45] McGinnis, Maura. *Greece: A Primary Source Cultural Guide.* 2003.

[46] Baker, Rosalie F. and Charles F. Baker III. *Ancient Greeks: Creating the Classical Tradition.* 1997.

built using new technology that came from the Corinthians, who had adopted it from the Phoenicians.[47]

The trireme galley, fitted with three sections of rowers, came into fashion for military purposes by that time. These large ships required 85 rowers on each side to function, but additional rowers were often added in the middle rows to add more power to the oars.[48] Under the power of so much muscle, the trireme was faster at its top rowing speed than any other ship under sail. It was perfect for quick attacks and shortened international journeys, be they for military gain or trade purposes. Often, the feudal kings of these ancient port cities and burgeoning empires forewent trade altogether in favor of attacking their neighbor for territorial gains, thus raiding the enemy cities for supplies and hauling anything of use back home.

Though they'd only just come out of a war, the Athenians were wary of the cost of such an endeavor. The project was put off for seven years, which is when the city discovered an incredibly valuable stock of silver buried in Attica.[49]

Democratically, of course, the Athenian archons gathered together to discuss what to do with all that silver. Most of them wanted to split it among themselves, but Themistocles stepped up onto the podium with his radical idea of spending the silver on a trireme fleet. It was the best thing to do, the general explained, so that Athens would be protected from its enemies in the nearby city-state of Aegina.[50] The Aeginians were island people with the strongest seafaring vessels and mariners in the realm, and they had a long-standing rivalry with mainland Athens. By appealing to this deeply embedded rivalry, Themistocles succeeded in gaining the popular vote for his navy building project.

---

[47] Thucydides. *History of the Peloponnesian War.*

[48] Jordan, Borimir. "The Crews of Athenian Triremes." 2000.

[49] Pritchard, David M. *Athenian Democracy at War.* 2018.

[50] PBS. "483 BC – Athens Builds a Navy."

It was none too soon, since King Xerxes I, the new power in Persia after the death of his father, had just vowed to burn Athens to the ground.[51] He began gathering his forces, and news of the impending attack reached Athens soon afterward. In a panic, the people sent an urgent query to the gods at the Oracle of Delphi, asking what might be done to protect the city. The Oracle responded with an alarming message: "Why sit you, doomed one? Fly to the ends of the earth. All is ruin for fire and headlong god of war shall bring you low."[52]

The Athenians were horrified, but Themistocles, who had been preparing for another attack ever since the Persians were defeated a decade before, sent his own query to the Oracle and received the following response: "Though all else shall be taken, Zeus, the all-seeing, grants that the wooden wall only shall not fail."[53]

The message was confusing to all but Themistocles. The "wooden wall" could be none other than the fleet of triremes constructed of wooden timbers. Unsure what else to do, the Athenians followed the guidance of their general and evacuated the city. Soldiers and rowers climbed into the boats while their wives, mothers, and children fled to a nearby village. The city was completely abandoned when Xerxes' army marched in and set it aflame, just as the Persian king had promised. The temples, markets, homes, and public buildings were all destroyed, but the Athenian army lay in wait safely on Salamis. They would have been able to see the smoke rising from their wasted city.[54]

The other Greek city-states had sent their own smaller fleets to Salamis to rendezvous with the Athenians, and under the orders of the Spartan general Eurybiades, they waited for the Persian ships to

---

[51] King, Perry Scott. *Pericles*. 1987.

[52] Place, Robert M. *Astrology and Divination*. 2009.

[53] Ibid.

[54] Bauer, Susan Wise. *The History of the Ancient World*. 2007.

enter the narrow Strait of Salamis. There, in a tiny strait of the sea, Themistocles and Eurybiades hoped to engage the enemy in battle.[55] The boats of the enemy were no match for the Greek fleet of triremes in such small quarters. To lure the Persians into the trap, Themistocles sent a messenger to Xerxes, claiming that he was defecting to Persia. The messenger told Xerxes where he could find the Greek ships and attack while they were unprepared.[56] Xerxes believed the messenger and ordered his fleet to row through the night, aiming for the southern end of the strait. There, he found an orderly line of Athenian triremes at the ready.

The triremes attacked, using their narrow shape and lightness to pummel the sides of the enemy ships. The playwright, Aeschylus, fought alongside his fellow Athenians and lived to write the epic tale in his play, *The Persians*.

> We heard from every part, his voice of exultation. "Advance, ye sons of Greece! From slavery, save your country! Save your wives; your children, save! This day, the common cause of all demands your valor!"

King Xerxes watched the battle unfold from his golden throne on the shore of the mainland and saw the Greeks destroy 200 of his boats.[57] The Persians retreated after heavy losses and fled home to protect their king and recover. For the first time in history, Athenians knew what it felt like to be truly powerful. The survivors went back to their ruined city and began to rebuild.

---

[55] Strauss, Barry. *The Battle of Salamis.*

[56] Ferrill, Arthur. *The Origins of War Revised Edition.* 2018.

[57] **"Greek-Persian Wars (490 BCE–479 BCE)."** Gale Encyclopedia of World History: War. *Encyclopedia.com.*

Chapter 6 – Slavery

To celebrate their incredible victory over the best of the Persian Empire, Athens declared itself a fully democratic and sovereign realm. This was by no means an unprecedented move, of course, given that Athenian rulers had already created a somewhat democratic system that had been in use for many years. It was the goal of many within the government, however, to improve that system for the betterment of all Athenians. In any case, the city proudly brandished its democratic ideologies in the face of its tyrannical enemies. And yet, slavery remained a fundamental cog in the Athenian machine.

The ancient Greeks practiced slavery as if it were a natural part of the human experience. Even Aristotle, a great philosopher born a century afterward, still believed that it was necessary for humans to rule over other humans to establish a sensible order.[58] The definition of an Athenian citizen was mostly based on the discrimination of women, immigrants, and slaves. To qualify for Athenian citizenship, one had to be a male of at least eighteen years in age with two Athenian-born parents.[59] Such restrictive citizenship meant that

---

[58] Aristotle. *Politics.*

[59] Phillips, David. *The Law of Ancient Athens.* 2013.

slaves largely outnumbered voting Athenians.[60] Slaves were mostly foreigners from other Greek kingdoms, having been subjugated under the conquering armies of Athens or bought outright from local merchants.[61]

Athenian slaves were perhaps the most civilly treated in all of Hellas, as it was frequently noted by outsiders that:

> ...the Athenians allow their slaves to live in a lap of luxury, and some of them indeed live in a life of real magnificence, this too is something that they can be seen to do with good reason. For where power is based on the navy, because of the need for money there is no choice but to end up enslaved to slaves, so that we can take a share of their earnings, and to let them go free...This is why in the matter of freedom of speech we have put slaves on equal terms with free men, and [former slaves] with citizens, for the city needs [former slaves] because of all its skilled activities and because of the fleet.[62]

Athenians used their slaves for many purposes. Many of the slave women provided household cooking and cleaning services for their masters or were sent to state-run brothels to work. Large numbers of captive slaves were taken from conquered lands en masse and put to work in the rock quarries and silver mines.[63] Hundreds at a time, from conquered neighboring realms, were taken to Athens and given civil duties. They were instructed to form a police force within Athens, to build public edifices and new homes, or work the farmland.[64]

---

[60] Sansone, David. *Ancient Greek Civilization.* 2016.

[61] Wilson, Nigel Guy. *Encyclopedia of Ancient Greece.* 2006.

[62] Fuller, Roslyn. *Beasts and Gods: How Democracy Changed Its Meaning and Lost Its Purpose.* 2015.
[63] Lauffer, S. "Die Bergwerkssklaven von Laureion," *Abhandlungen* no.12. 1956.

[64] Miller, Margaret C. *Athens and Persia in the Fifth Century BC.* 2004.

Indeed, anyone who worked in manual labor in Athens was either a slave or a poor citizen. Free men with the means to own slaves sent them to perform the necessary work of the day while they put their minds to philosophy, art, architectural design, and above all, politics. Pericles, a popular statesman of Athens during its Golden Age, once remarked that a man who did not bother to think on matters of the state was beyond apathetic—he was useless.[65] The practice of self-government was very important to Athenians. Women, foreigners, and slaves were not destined to become a part of this system, however.

Athenian men of means enjoyed the ultimate of luxuries in that they had the time and wherewithal to pursue entertainment and philosophy. They loved music, dance, and art, and they made sure their children were taught to play a musical instrument. Usually, this was the lyre, an ancient precursor to the guitar. Dancers were generally enslaved women, as were the musicians and even those responsible for piecing together Athens' famous mosaic artworks.[66] Citizens who felt a particular passion for music or art also took part in exhibitions. When the men weren't enjoying a show, they were often found debating politics.

Naturally, this left the infrastructure of Athens in the hands of its imported slaves, and they complied, having very little choice. Female slaves mostly took on household jobs of food preparation, maintenance, cleaning, and child care, while the men were sent to do hard labor in the fields, mines, and quarries. Not all male slaves suffered in the fields or rock pits, however. Since Athens' slave population included many educated men who had been stolen from

[65] Kagan, Donald. *Pericles of Athens and the Birth of Democracy.* 1998.

[66] Carr, K.E. "Greek slaves: What was it like to be a slave in ancient Greece?". Quatr.us Study Guides, July 12, 2017. Web. March 20, 2019.

their lands, these men were put to work as guards, police, teachers, doctors, shopkeepers, and personal ancillaries. [67]

It was considered best practice for slave owners to keep their male and female slaves apart and in separate quarters to better control any fraternization and sexual relationships that could lead to children.[68] Unlike other slave-owning societies, the Athenians did not try to breed their own race of bonded workers; still, it was not uncommon for female slaves to give birth while in service to a citizen or family. These children were kept as the property of the household, but they usually enjoyed greater freedoms than their parents. Born slaves were entrusted with the entire welfare of the household's free children, and even their financial records and savings.[69] To have a slave as your accountant was not a strange thing to an ancient Athenian.

Wealthy citizens could amass great numbers of personal slaves which they used to provide extra income for their own households. A rich Greek would lease his slaves to the city or army and thereby make a comfortable and passive income. In a civilization without monetary currency (at least until the 6th century BCE), one's slaves served as a measure of his wealth. The more slaves you owned, the more work could be done; the more goods procured and sold, the more rent you could earn from leasing them out. Economically speaking, slave ownership was more indicative of a man's importance and influence in a city more than money is today. The Athenian government was also a slave-owning body which generally used its holdings to populate the army.

---

[67] Medema, Stephen, and Warren J. Samuels. *Historians of Economics and Economic Thought.* 2001.

[68] Lambert, S. D. (editor.) *Sociable Man.* 2011.

[69] Carr, K.E. "Greek slaves: What was it like to be a slave in ancient Greece?" Quatr.us Study Guides, July 12, 2017. Web. March 20, 2019.

With no distinct differences in the physical features of slaves and citizens, and no distinct clothing to separate the two, it was not easy to know right away who was enslaved or not. Most slaves wore a simple, short white tunic called a chiton, which was also considered appropriate dress for citizens and women alike. It was much easier to pinpoint members of the wealthier families since their fashions more often included brightly colored tunics and cloaks. Dyed cloth was more expensive than plain linen, so it was only used by the aristocracy.

Athenian slaves may have been among the best treated in history, but they were still under the dominion of their masters and subject to beatings. Such behavior was not considered civilized by most citizens, even though the laws of the city mostly allowed for this. There were several specificities when it came to the law and violence against the enslaved. If a citizen inflicted harm onto the slave of another, the owner was in his rights to sue for damages. Conversely, a citizen could be taken to court for beating his slave too hard; he would also be sentenced to death if the individual he'd beaten died.[70]

It was not impossible for an Athenian slave to remove his or her bonds, and some households actually allowed for their slaves to save money for the eventual purchase of their freedom.[71] It was, however, very rare that a freeman was granted the full rights of a citizen of Athens.

[70] Carlier, P. *Le IVe siècle grec jusqu'à la mort d'Alexandre.* 1995; Aeschines, "Against Timarchus."

[71] Winer, Bart. *Life in the Ancient World.* 1961.

Chapter 7 – The Golden Age of Athens

Just because you do not take an interest in politics doesn't mean politics won't take an interest in you.

(Pericles)

Athens enjoyed what has been called its golden age after the expulsion of the Persians. Once the soldiers, women, and children returned to their new homes of their razed city, they enjoyed a period of economic growth, sports, arts, and continued democracy. Themistocles' navy remained the biggest and most powerful in the eastern Mediterranean, and Athens had become the reigning influence among its fellow Greek city-states. It was the end of the Archaic period and the beginning of the Classical period in Greece.

Within the Greek states, trade flourished between cities of all sizes. The Athenian port, in particular, was flooded with all manner of goods, including ox hides, mackerel, salted fish, ivory, rugs, cushions, and, of course, slaves. Thanks to such a wide array of food and goods, the quality of life for the average Athenian shot up. It was a wonderful time to live in Athens, whether one was a merchant, teacher, artisan, fisherman, soldier, or metal craftsman.

Though women were still not given the same rights as male citizens of Athens, the city prided itself on maintaining a democratic form of government. Citizens voted on their various magistrates, officials, and city leaders regularly. In addition to giving their support to specific citizens, voters had the chance to sentence one person to exile each year. This particular referendum election was conducted by having citizens write the name of a chosen person on a pottery shard, then submitting it into a large pot to be counted. Whoever's name appeared the most was banished from Athens.[72] It may seem superficial, but there was an ideological purpose to the annual banishment; if a person had become to be a threatening presence in the city—either politically or socially—he could be removed.

Ironically, the savior of Athens himself was targeted by his fellow citizens and ostracized entirely after his name dominated the exile voting: Themistocles.[73] Historians theorize that the war hero was the victim of a fixed election since archaeologists have recovered some of the damning pot shards bearing his name hoarded away.[74] Were they pre-prepared to stuff the counting pots? Or were these merely collected by an enthusiastic rival of Themistocles as a memento of his exile? It is difficult to know exactly what happened during the vote of 472/471 BCE, but the result was the same: Themistocles was banished. He retreated to Argos and eventually went to live in Persia, dying in the realm of the empire he'd once so heartily opposed.

In the political vacuum left by the absence of Themistocles, the Athenians turned to a new face: Pericles. Born into one of the most aristocratic families in Athens, his outlook for the city went far

[72] Sacks, David, and Oswyn Murray. *A Dictionary of the Ancient Greek World.* 1995.

[73] Thucydides. *The Landmark.*

[74] Forsdyke, Sara. *Exile, Ostracism, and Democracy.* 2009.

beyond internal governance and military adequacy. Pericles saw that the growing city was capable of much more than simply defending itself from empires. Athens itself could become a powerful empire if only the right person was at the helm. Pericles considered himself the right man to lead Athens to greatness.

He began by seeing that the old, burned, and ruined buildings of Athens were rebuilt even more grandly than they had been before Xerxes had sacked the city. The crucible of his rebuilding plan was the reconstruction of Athens' great Acropolis—a central area of beauty, pantheon worship, and public service. He would reconstruct it as a testament to the longevity, culture, and greatness of Athens. The most important buildings of the old Acropolis, including the Parthenon and Temple of Athena Nike, were rebuilt even bigger than before and in pure marble. It was the crowning glory of Athens, perched on a flat peak in the middle of the city.[75]

The completed Parthenon, a temple dedicated to Athena, was the most stunning building in all of Greece. Inside, a giant statue of the goddess of wisdom and war stood towering over all who entered. It was completed in only fifteen years, a true testament to the amazing skill and fortitude of the Athenian craftsmen involved in the project.[76]Pericles himself received all the praise for the new Acropolis, and as the city's leader, he basked in the acclaim. He hosted lavish dinner parties for the city's most beloved personalities, from mathematicians and astronomers to poets and historians. The power of his position affected his personal life and saw him divorce his first wife to cohabitate with a prostitute whose name was Aspasia.[77]

Prostitution was not looked upon quite the same way in ancient Athens as it is by most societies today. Aspasia considered herself a

---

[75] PBS. "447 BC – The Acropolis Rebuilt." Web.

[76] PBS. "The Buildings of the Acropolis." Web.

[77] Ostwald, M. *Athens as a Cultural Center.* 1992.

companion by trade and continued to do so even after moving into the home of her patron. The Athenians called women like her hetaera, and men hired their services as companions as well as prostitutes.[78] Unlike the wives of most men, hetaera like Aspasia were well-educated, independent, tax-paying members of the cities in which they lived. Women such as Aspasia were some of the only females in the Greek realm who enjoyed a reasonable amount of personal choice in the course of their lives. Aspasia herself even earned the respect of many of Athens' most affluent and intellectual men, her husband included. When Pericles and his wife received guests at their home, Aspasia was not expected to make a graceful and quiet exit when the men began to talk of philosophy and politics.

Pericles, Aspasia, and their friends were enthusiastic supporters of a burgeoning form of entertainment in those days—the theater. Twice a year, they attended what may be the world's first public theater, in Athens. Seated in solid marble chairs carved and polished to resemble lush textiles, Pericles and Aspasia watched the comedies of Aristophanes, the historical renderings of Aeschylus, and the tragedies of Sophocles and Euripides. The tragic plays were a favorite of all Athenians, who openly wept together in their seats. Greeks were not a particularly respectful audience, however, and if they did not like certain actors or characters, they would boo and hiss until he left the performance altogether.[79]

Popular works by these playwrights stunned and entranced audiences, playing on the people's natural tendency to appreciate sadness, tragedy, empathy, and malice. They adored shocking stories such as that of the King Oedipus, who gouged out his own eyes after the discovery that his new wife was in truth his long-lost mother. Or King Agamemnon, who returned home after the ten-year Trojan War only to be murdered by his wife's lover.

---

[78] **"Aspasia: Influential Concubine to Pericles."** *Ancient History Encyclopedia.* Last modified January 18, 2012.

[79] Kennedy, Dennis. *The Oxford Companion to Theatre and Performance.* 2010.

Pericles' Athens was characterized by the theater, great thinkers, beauty, and architectural and mathematical feats that were rarely equaled in other cities and empires of the ancient world. Not unlike the Acropolis that stood shining on the pedestal of Athens, so too did Golden Age Athens sit on the metaphorical pedestal of all Greece. Alas, it could not last.

Chapter 8 – Pericles at War

Themistocles' navy was the envy of all Greece, and its establishment prompted similar investments in trireme building throughout the Mediterranean. The most powerful leaders of city-states and kingdoms along the sea conducted their crews back and forth over the water, raiding one city and peacefully trading with the next, until the waters of the Mediterranean were filled with large galleys, soldiers, merchants, and intrepid travelers searching for knowledge and adventure. Life sped up and multiplied rapidly in this little corner of the universe until urban communities became the powerhouses of the landscape.

It was as it had been centuries before in Ionia and the small, peaceful towns of Greece and Anatolia: The number of wealthy families grew so that whole scores of citizens were able to spend time thinking and wondering about their place in the bigger picture that was life. Thus, spiritual enlightenment and the intellectual pursuit of knowledge came to define an entire civilization. Pericles saw all this happening in his Athenian home, and it inspired him to turn Athens into the next Babylon.

Themistocles and Pericles had transformed the once humble democratic city into a beautiful, well-fortified center of military prowess, intellect, trade, and luxury. Still, it was not enough for Pericles. He desired nothing less than an Athenian empire, and once he felt the city's internal structure was the envy of all of Greece, Pericles knew it was time to act. He also knew exactly how empires were won—through ruthless warfare. Having helped his fellow citizens to build the most enviable culture of the 5th-century BCE Greek world, he now persuaded them to fight for the ideals of Athens on the battlefields of foreign nations.

First, Pericles had to deal with Athens' nearest adversary: Sparta. Tensions had risen between the two realms ever since they had banded together as allies within the Hellenic League. As strong as Athens had become, its elected leaders knew better than to think theirs was an infallible city. They formed the Hellenic League to consolidate the culture and sovereignty of 300 Greek cities, including Athens and Sparta.[80] This Greek alliance meant a larger navy, more military resources, and, above all, no more infighting among the cities of the realm. Now, their focus was targeted outward, toward the greater enemies of the world.

It was not a perfect solution. The Spartans were jealous of the Athenian monopoly over the League, while Athenians felt superior over the military power in the south. It was not difficult to goad either side into war against the other, especially since Greek culture was by nature one that glorified warriors over all others.

Spartan King Archidamus II made the first move by invading Attica in 431 BCE.[81] Pericles took action, convincing all Athenians to retreat behind the fortified stone walls of the city proper, which stretched all the way down to the port at Piraeus.[82] Though cut off by land from external resources, Pericles determined to keep the port

---

[80] Gray, Colin S. and Roger W. Barnett. *Seapower and Strategy.* 1989.

[81] Balot, Ryan K; Forsdyke, Sara; and Edith Foster editors. *The Oxford Handbook of Thucydides.* 2017.

[82] Conwell, David. *Connecting a City to the Sea.* 2008.

open to merchant suppliers thanks to extensive fortifications around the entire harbor, including archer's towers. Though the walls may be put to siege, Pericles was confident that the port would not fail. The city prepared to stay in confinement for as many as three years, expecting that Sparta's forces would wear thin or admit defeat before more time passed. While the population of Attica shrank back behind the city walls and waited for their leader's prediction to come to pass, Pericles sent the navy to attack the Spartan coastline known as the Peloponnesian coast. This military campaign between Athens and Sparta came to be known as the Peloponnesian War.

As the great citizens of the beautiful city sheltered alongside one another, doing their best to pass the time in an entertaining—if not particularly productive—manner. Pericles hosted lavish dinner parties with all the intellectuals of the day. Renown philosopher and oddball Socrates amused his host and friends at such parties by making eloquent speeches in favor of his own beauty over that of others.[83] In reality, Socrates knew all too well that his face was anything but lovely, but he did not mind poking fun at himself for the benefit of a laugh or a good debate. He always strove to teach those among him to learn by asking questions and follow their own good judgment.

"I tell you, let no day pass without discussing all the things about which you hear me talking. A life without this sort of examination is not a life worth living," he told his friends and students.[84]

Outside the city walls, Spartan warriors occupied the Athenians' farmland, burning and slashing their crops, vines, and orchards.[85] After one year in the closed city, the port that was Athens' lifeline

---

[83] Lawrence, Joseph P. *Sócrates Among Strangers*. 2015. Note: Pericles and Socrates were contemporaries who almost certainly dined amongst one another multiple times, but Plato's recollection of his dialogue on beauty did not necessarily occur at the table of Pericles.

[84] Plato. *Apology*.

[85] Hanson, Victor Davis. *A War Like No Other*. 2011.

proved just as dangerous as the Spartans outside. It was 430 BCE when plague accompanied the goods that passed through Piraeus, infecting those within the fortified walls.[86] It was an ironic attack from an enemy against which no defensive measures had been—or could have been—taken. It was the worst possible time for such illness, as the Athenians were crowded behind their city walls and piled against one another. Conditions in the city were conducive only to quickening the disastrous spread of disease which struck its victims down rapidly.

Victims were first afflicted with what the historian Thucydides called "violent inflammation" of the head and eyes. Next, the illness moved into the gut, causing "ulceration and uncontrollable diarrhea." People died in sick, suffering heaps, and the birds and street animals who dared to eat the flesh of the corpses themselves suffered the same fate. It was catastrophic, with dead bodies piled in the stinking streets and nothing but imported and potentially infected goods coming through the port. Little did the Athenians know, the plague had begun in northern Africa and followed popular trade routes all the way into Piraeus, where it spent three long years agonizing the citizens of Athens. At least one-quarter of the city's population died in horrid pain, and Pericles was not spared.[87]

Plutarch, Pericles' biographer, described how the plague struck the city's beloved leader:

"The plague seized Pericles not with sharp and violent fits, but with dull and lingering distemper...wasting the strength of his body and undermining his noble soul."[88]

---

[86] Thucydides. *The Landmark.*

[87] Littman, R.J. "The Plague of Athens: Epidemiology and Paleopathology." 2009.

[88] Plutarch. *Life of Pericles.*

All manner of known medicines and miracle cures were administered to the suffering man, but after six months of illness, he too succumbed to the disease, dying in 429 BCE.

Political chaos followed the death of the great statesman as multiple politicians jostled for the vote of the citizens. With no clear leadership and mob rule threatening to overrun the city, Athenian soldiers found themselves ordered about at the whims of an unprepared group of leaders who quickly abandoned Pericles' war strategies. Pericles himself had died surrounded by friends who praised his many achievements; his war, however, was lost. Athens surrendered in 404 BCE and became a subject of the new powerhouse of Greece, Sparta.[89]

---

[89] Del Re, Gerard and Patricia Del Re. *History's Last Stand.* 1993.

Chapter 9 – The Socratic Method

The only true wisdom is in knowing you know nothing.

(Socrates)

As far as the philosophers and intellectuals of Classical Antiquity were concerned, the pillar of their own enlightened civilization was the great thinker Socrates—the ugly, outlandish war hero whose ideas on social reform forever transformed Western culture. He was an unlikely hero, a humble man who wore no shoes and rarely attended the Athenian Assembly to participate in politics. Amazingly, the man never wrote any of his own philosophies and theories down, so our only link to Socrates himself is through the writings of other men whom he influenced. The principal among these are Plato and Xenophon, his students.

Born in about 470 BCE in Athens, Socrates was an important part of the city's Golden Age.[90] His most influential theory concerned that of wisdom and philosophy itself. He believed that true knowledge only comes from within; to try to pass wisdom from person to person, he said, was indoctrination, not real intelligence. It was probably for this very reason that he did not become an author since

---

[90] Lim, Jun. *Sócrates: The Public Conscience of Golden Age Athens.* 2006.

he did not simply want to pass his own worldview on to the next generation. Instead, Socrates wanted the people of Athens to make their own realizations about reality. Only that, he argued, was real truth and knowledge.

It was strange for a teacher not to supply his students with a set of facts or correct answers, but in encouraging his pupils to find their own path to the answers they sought, Socrates lay the foundations of Western philosophy. Even today, philosophical schools define themselves as institutions that teach students how to think. The Socratic method is the incredible, lasting legacy of a man whose own words we cannot possibly know.

In Socrates' time, Athenian education catered only to young males from about the age of seven and focused on physical and literary topics.[91] Boys spent much of their time in a gymnasium learning to play games and wrestle. The purpose of their physical exertion was twofold: the Greeks valued the beauty of strong young men with lean limbs, but they also needed such men to populate the army which was constantly engaged in domestic defense. When the boys were not participating in physical education, they learned to read and write using the Greek alphabet. They practiced writing on tablets coated in wax, on which they etched their letters with a stylus, and memorized literature written by Homer and other more contemporary poets.[92]

Girls were educated by their mothers or female family members at home. They learned how to care for the house and children but only learned to read or write if their parents employed a private tutor.[93] This did not change much in the following centuries, but the education of young men changed quite dramatically in the 5th

[91] Beaumont, Leslie. *Childhood in Ancient Athens.* 2013.

[92] Sacks, David; Murray, Oswyn; and Lisa R. Brody. *Encyclopedia of the Ancient Greek World.* 2014.

[93] Laurin, Joseph R. *The Life of Women in Ancient Athens.* 2013.

century BCE thanks to the influence of Socrates and his own students. Higher education was born, catering to the young adult male student who had already mastered his letters, music lessons, and poetry memorizations. There was a fundamental shift in Athenian culture where the younger generations began to respect intelligence and education over physical strength. Socrates' own students would have learned logic and rhetoric from their lessons while being taught arithmetic and musical harmonics from other tutors.

Plato is our main source of Socratic thought and method, thanks to his extensive works on the subject of thought and knowledge. Plato featured his teacher in at least four books that were written after the death of Socrates: *Symposium*, *Apology*, *Crito*, and *Phaedo*. In these works, Socrates heartily refuses to accept money in exchange for his lessons; he did not want to be considered a teacher. In fact, he took pride in the poverty of his station, believing that it belied true wisdom and morality. As a thought leader and teacher of the sons of noble families, Socrates was a controversial figure amongst his contemporaries. For every person in Greece who considered him wise, there was another who thought him blasphemous and guilty of polluting the minds of the youth.

Indeed, Socrates was brought to trial for his alleged disrespect of the gods and his corruption of Athenian youth in 399 BCE.[94] His students were appalled at the turn of events. In *Memorabilia*, Xenophon wrote:

> I have often wondered by what arguments the accusers of Socrates persuaded the Athenians that he deserved death from the state; for the indictment against him was to this effect: Socrates offends against the laws in not paying respect to those gods whom the city respects and introducing other

---

[94] Cartledge, Paul. *Ancient Greek Political Thought in Practice.* 2009.

new deities; he also offends against the laws in corrupting the youth.

In the first place, that he did not respect the gods whom the city respects, what proof did they bring? For he was seen frequently sacrificing at home, and frequently on the public altars of the city; nor was it unknown that he used divination; as it was a common subject of talk that "Socrates used to say that the divinity instructed him;" and it was from this circumstance, indeed, that they seem chiefly to have derived the charge of introducing new deities.

Despite the support of many Athenians, Socrates was ultimately found guilty of these crimes and sentenced to death by way of a poison hemlock drink. According to Plato and Xenophon, Socrates took the drink without a fuss and covered his face while awaiting death. His last words were almost certainly meant in irony: "Crito, we owe a debt to Asclepius. Pay it and do not neglect it."[95]

The students of Socrates ensured that his legacy lived on; Plato carefully documented his teacher's most inspiring dialogues and histories and in turn educated the next generation of Athenian students using the Socratic method. His school, the Academy, was founded in around 387 BCE.[96]

---

[95] Xenophon. *The Memorabilia of Xenophon.* Note: These words made mention of the god of medicine, who theoretically would have been responsible for helping prepare the hemlock drink. As Socrates had been found guilty of blasphemy against the gods, he probably said this facetiously.

[96] Kramer, Hans Joachim. *Plato and the Foundations of Metaphysics.* 1990.

Chapter 10 - Plato

In politics we presume that everyone who knows how to get votes knows how to administer a city or a state. When we are ill...we do not ask for the handsomest physician, or the most eloquent one.

(Plato)

Plato was born in about 428 BCE in Athens.[97] At the feet of Socrates, he studied philosophy, mathematics, and the sciences. Greatly inspired by the work of his teacher and Pythagoras, Plato went to great lengths to obtain a copy of Pythagoras' work so that he could study the great philosopher's mathematics and personal ideologies firsthand and use them as a foundation for his own work.[98] He'd been inspired to do so after meeting a group of people who emulated the lifestyle of Pythagoras, from his diet to his communal home. To Plato, Pythagoras was as important to mankind as the Titan Prometheus had been when he brought humans the gift of fire.

---

[97] Brown, Calvin. *Masterworks of World Literature.* 1970.

[98] Bernard, Raymond W. *Pythagoras, the Immortal Sage.* 1958.

Plato's most well-known literary work, *The Republic*, describes an egalitarian community very much like the one championed by Pythagoras less than a century before. This wasn't Plato's only extension of Pythagoras' work; he also took his predecessor's studies of the stars and the theory of a round Earth and perfected it, positing that the Earth spun on an axis at the center of the universe.[99]

In philosophical endeavors, Plato was fixated on the theme of love. It was not an uncommon philosophical pursuit in Classical Greece, but Plato's musings on the subject have come to define the many types of loving emotions that humans are naturally inclined to experience during their lives. Nearly his entire book *Symposium* is made up of a set of monologues on love. He included Socrates as the main character, providing readers with a valuable glimpse into the life and habits of one of Western civilization's first philosophers. This was a common feature in Plato's literature, the many dialogues between Socrates and other important citizens of Athens. The term "platonic love" has been used to describe the non-sexual types of love Plato discusses in his books.

In honor of Socrates, Plato founded the first institute of higher learning in Athens called the Academy, and he taught his students to employ the Socratic method of exploration and experimentation. He took this very seriously; above the door of the Academy were the Greek words "Let no one enter here who is ignorant of geometry."[100] Plato wanted his students to come prepared with a basic education upon which they would be able to build up to more advanced subjects. He encouraged students to ask questions about their lessons and then formulate hypotheses based on the information they put together. They would test their theories and either move forward based on positive results or start again if their hypothesis was negated. Another of Plato's philosophical methods was that of

---

[99] Plato. *Timaeus*. Note: Plato's astronomical theories have been interpreted in various ways, one of which is used here.

[100] Rosen, Stanley. *The Philosopher's Handbook.* 2009.

dialectic discussion, in which several opposing points of view are used in a discussion to establish a universal truth between them.[101]

The theory of forms is an excellent example of how Plato's philosophical models of thinking revolutionized traditional thought patterns. He posited that we could think of each object or idea in two forms: the phenomenon and the ideal. This is demonstrated in his "Allegory of the Cave," a model described by Socrates in Plato's *Republic*. In the Allegory, several prisoners sit chained, facing the back of a large cave. Behind them is a roadway leading toward the exit, and beyond that is a large fire. Since the prisoners can only face one direction, they see the incorrect forms of reality in the black shadows before them. Whatever true form passes between the prisoners and the fire is misconstrued in those shadows which are all the people can ever perceive.

The philosopher, explained Socrates via Plato, is one who has been unbound from his place in that cave. He can now turn around and discover the light from the fire—surely a metaphor for universal truth.

---

[101] Gonzales, Francisco J. *Dialetic and Dialogue*. 1998.

Chapter 11 – Alexander the Great

I imitate Herakles, and emulate Perseus, and follow in the footsteps of Dionysos, the divine author and progenitor of my family, and desire that victorious Hellenes should dance again in India and revive the memory of the Bacchic revels among the savage mountain tribes beyond the Kaukasos...

(Alexander the Great, as quoted in Plutarch's *On the Fortune or the Virtue of Alexander*)

Socrates and his students were products of their environment, in that they had the time and means to consider their place in the wider world and the universe at large. In a book attributed to him entitled *Magna Moralia*, Plato's student, Aristotle, explains to his readers how it was due to Socrates that modern Athenians valued knowledge over physical prowess. As committed to spreading Socratic philosophy and knowledge as Plato had been, Aristotle founded his own school in Athens called Lyceum.[102] At the behest of King Philip II of Macedon, he became a tutor to the king's 13-year-old son, Prince Alexander.[103]

---

[102] Lynch, John Patrick. *Aristotle's School.* 1972.

[103] Chandler, Joyce Helen. *Alexander the Man: King Alexander.* 2006.

Alexander inherited the kingdom of Macedon at the age of twenty when his father was assassinated in 336 BCE.[104] Though he was a young ruler, Alexander was more than capable of acting the part of a king. He was well trained in the arts of horsemanship and war but also well educated under the tutelage of his esteemed teacher, Aristotle.

Alexander's kingdom was everything that Pericles had hoped Athens could be. Though Macedon did conduct the majority of its business in the capital city of Pella, it was comprised of other cities, villages, and farms and therefore not entirely focused on its capital, as Athens was. Philip II had invaded the Greek city-states to the south just a few years previously, uniting almost every realm under Macedonian rule and giving himself and his son access to their formidable armies as part of the Hellenic League.[105] The Hellenic League was a unification of Greek realms that represented most of mainland and Aegean Greece under the leadership of the Kingdom of Macedon, including Athens but excluding Sparta. Alexander had a vast empire in mind just as Pericles had, and with the powerful Macedonian kingdom his father had built as his foundation, the young king found his dream quite achievable. He set out almost immediately upon his succession with a force of 40,000 soldiers to Thrace and then Thebes to quell the quick revolts that had sprung up against his rule.[106]

The new king was hesitant to march into Persia without first securing his own borders at home. His army dominated the Thracians and Illyrians to the north of Macedon, ensuring no rivalry there in the near future. He marched directly to Thebes thereafter, who had rebelled in tandem with Athens. Alexander and his troops all but destroyed Thebes, causing Athens to cautiously abandon its

---

[104] Ibid.

[105] Gabriel, Richard A. *Phillip II of Macedonia: Greater than Alexander.* 2010.

[106] Wenkart, Michael. *The 50 Most Influential People in History.* 2014.

own revolutionary plans.[107] Satisfied that the home front was secure, Alexander marched eastward and left his trusted General Antipater as regent of Macedon and Commander of the League of Corinth (another name for the Hellenic League).[108]

In addition to his 40,000 soldiers, Alexander took 120 warships from Crete with the same number of men across the Aegean Sea into Persia.[109] His first clash with the Persian forces was victorious, so he continued southeast along the eastern edge of the Aegean coast, freeing the Greek cities there who had been ruled by the Persians since the days of King Xerxes, granting them the right to practice democracy under his leadership.[110, 111] His next stop was the Persian city of Gordium, where he intended to write himself into local legend.

Centuries earlier, Gordium had been the capital of the Kingdom of Phrygia. Legend has it that the Phrygians—possibly descended from nomadic Thracians—had found themselves without leadership and could not decide on who among them should be crowned king.[112, 113] In true Greek fashion, they consulted an oracle who told them the next man to drive into town with an ox-cart would be their king. They followed this advice and so ordained Gordias their king. His ox-cart was tied to a pole using an excessive multitude of complex

---

[107] Rawlings, Louis. *The Ancient Greeks at War.* 2007.

[108] Brice, Lee L. *Greek Warfare.* 2012.

[109] Trawinski, Allan. *The Clash of Civilizations.* 2017.

[110] Cartwright, Mark. **"Lydia."** *Ancient History Encyclopedia.* Ancient History Encyclopedia, 03 Apr 2016. Web. 21 Mar 2019.

[111] Nawotka, Krzysztof. (2003). "Freedom of Greek cities in Asia Minor in the age of Alexander the Great". 85. 15-41.

[112] Tuna, Numan; Akture Zeynep; and Maggie Lynch. *Thracians and Phrygians: Problems of Parallelism.* 1998.

[113] Gilbert, Samuel L. *The Riemann Hypothesis.* 2009.

knots, and there it stayed until Alexander of Macedon happened upon it.[114]

Any man who could unfasten the knot, the oracle had said, was destined to rule all of Asia. Alexander determined that man would be himself. He tried pulling at various sections of the ancient knot but saw that it was futile and instead brandished his sword. Slashing through the legendary Gordian Knot, the young emperor proclaimed that it mattered not how the knot was loosed so long as the problem had been solved.[115]

In 333 BCE, the Greek army faced Darius III, named in honor of the father of King Xerxes, the man whose forces were defeated by Themistocles and the Athenians at sea.[116] After prolonged fighting between the two kings' armies, Darius fled and left his own army in disarray, along with his wife and mother.[117] Alexander was victorious once more. After dividing up the conquered lands under the administrative rule of his allies, the young warlord made his way to Egypt via a very reluctant Gaza.

Amazingly, the Egyptians welcomed Alexander and his conquering army with open arms, the priests of Memphis happily anointing him their chosen king.[118] Though the Macedonian's moniker was King of Asia for besting the Gordian Knot, it was the political annexation of Egypt under Greek rule that seemed to give him the most pride. He spent six months in the new Macedonian province, laying the groundwork for his brand-new city of Alexandria and meeting with

---

[114] Ibid.

[115] Note: According to Plutarch, the popular tale of Alexander slicing through the knot with his sword is incorrect. Plutarch insisted that the king separated the knot from its fastenings by pulling out a pole pin.

[116] Green, Peter. *Alexander of Macedon: 356-323 B.C.* 1991.

[117] Ibid.

[118] Ibid.

local diplomats and governors.[119] During his time in Egypt, Alexander organized a cultural and sports festival whose feats and exhibitions celebrated both Egyptian and Greek civilizations. Alexander's vision for Egypt was that of the most modern society— a mixture of Greeks and Egyptians who valued higher learning, architectural beauty, and, of course, military might.

The time came when the Greeks were finally compelled to leave Egypt, and on their way home, they claimed Babylon and even lay claim to a large swathe of the Indus River Valley in India.[120] He came away with several thousand war elephants with which to terrorize the Middle and Far East. Unfortunately, by that point, his army had had enough. They were wary of the massive forces of the Nanda Empire awaiting them in the southern portions of India and were eager to go home and enjoy the fruits of their 12-year labor.[121] Facing mutiny, Alexander was convinced to return to Greece at long last. Alas, he did not make it that far.

In June of 323 BCE, Alexander of Macedon died following a sudden illness. Several accounts of his death survive, many of which suggest that the king was poisoned in the same fashion as his dear friend, Hephaestion, who died shortly before.[122] Alexander died in Babylon, but his mummified corpse was sealed in a golden sarcophagus and sent to Macedon.[123] En route, the sarcophagus was intercepted by Ptolemy I Soter who brought it to Memphis; Ptolemy II Philadelphus

[119] Skelton, Debra, and Pamela Dell. *Empire of Alexander the Great.* 2009.

[120] Ibid.

[121] Muehlbauer, Matthew S. and David J. Ulbrich (editors.) *The Routledge History of Global War and Society.* 2018.

[122] Heckel, Waldemar and Lawrence A. Tritle (editors.) *Alexander the Great: A New History.* 2011,

[123] Robert S. Bianchi. "Hunting Alexander's Tomb". Archaeology.org. 2004.

later brought it to Alexandria, where it remained on public display for all of Classical Antiquity.[124]

By the 4th century CE, the location of the tomb was no longer known. Extensive searches for Alexander's remains have been fruitlessly conducted ever since.[125]

---

[124] Ibid.

[125] Ibid.

Chapter 12 – The Hellenistic Period

The educated differ from the uneducated as much as the living differ from the dead.

(Aristotle)[126]

The years following the death of Alexander the Great were politically chaotic but also quite decadent for citizens of Greece proper. Though portions of the new lands acquired by Alexander returned to local rule, the empire still remained massive.[127] It was divided into four realms, each ruled by one of Alexander's own military generals. Egypt, Cyprus, and part of the Middle East went to Ptolemy I; Seleucus I Nicator ruled Babylon, Persia, and Alexander's holdings in India; Lysimachus took Thrace and the western section of Asia; and Cassander took Macedon and Greece.[128,129]

---

[126] Quoted by Diogenes in *Sayings and Anecdotes: with Other Popular Moralists.*

[127] Green, P. *Alexander the Great and the Hellenistic Age.* 2007.

[128] Mark, Joshua J. "The Hellenistic World: The World of Alexander the Great." *Ancient History Encyclopedia.* Ancient History Encyclopedia, 01 Nov 2018. Web. 21 Mar 2019.

However, the former Macedonian emperor was not childless. His wife, the Bactrian Princess Roxana, was pregnant at the time of Alexander's death, and therefore, his potential direct heir could not yet lay claim to any of his father's lands. Born in August of 323 BCE, Alexander IV was proclaimed the true leader of the unbroken empire, and Antipater, Cassander's father, named himself regent. When Antipater died in 319, he appointed someone older and more experienced to succeed him.[130] This truly upset his son who started a war which he ultimately won in 317.[131] It is suspected that Cassander poisoned Alexander IV along with Roxana in 310, leaving only Heracles, the illegitimate son of Alexander the Great and his Persian mistress, potentially vying for power.[132, 133] He, too, was assassinated, and by 305 BCE, Cassander had declared himself King of Macedon.[134]

Cassander's rule was completely chaotic and unstable, and within a few years after his death, the Kingdom of Macedon fell to his enemy, Demetrius I, when the former's sons and heirs were killed in battle.[135] Demetrius had no use for democracy and made his own selections for the archons of Athens as well as other administrators of the realm.[136]

---

[129] Lightman, Marjorie and Benjamin Lightman. *A to Z of Ancient Greek and Roman Women.* 2008.

[130] Waterfield, Robin. *Dividing the Spoils.* 2012.

[131] Ibid.

[132] Geoffrey, Nicholas; Hammond, Lemprière; and Walbank, Frank William. *A History of Macedonia: 336-167 B.C.* 1988.

[133] Grant, David. *In Search of the Lost Testament of Alexander the Great.* 2017.

[134] Waterfield, Robin. *Dividing the Spoils.* 2012.

[135] Ibid.

[136] Shear, T. Leslie. *Kallias of Spettos and The Revolt of Athens in 286 B.C.* 1978.

Outside Greece proper, Alexander's conquered lands filled with Greek immigrants who sought new fortunes in the many cities their former emperor had founded along his warpath. The Egyptian Alexandria became a new haven of Egyptian-Greco culture, just as its founder had wished. It was a new age in the land of the pharaohs, one in which Greek-style philosophy and culture had become fashionable. The Ptolemaic Dynasty, ruled by descendants of a Macedonian general, was characterized by a Greek-style education with a focus on mathematics and science.[137] The Great Library of Alexandria was built during that time, and it was filled with texts from the great minds of the realm.

Alexander's ceaseless empire-building had succeeded in spreading Greek culture throughout the known world. In the self-named cities he'd founded, Greeks, Persians, Indians, and Arabs walked shoulder-to-shoulder, reading and writing in Greek and learning the mathematical wonders as discovered by Pythagoras.[138] They learned new philosophies using the Socratic method, and they became proud of their own education and sophistication over that of poorer—or what they considered barbaric—nations.

In about 280 BCE, the old Achaean League reunited, uniting the regions of southern Greece that lay adjacent to the Ionian Sea.[139] Within several decades, the group had grown to comprise all of southern Greece from the Ionian Sea to the Aegean Sea. The military might of the entire realm was greatly reduced by this period, and though its leaders maintained standing armies, they required the assistance of the Roman Republic in fighting the lengthy Macedonian Wars.[140]

---

[137] Professor Gerhard Rempel, *Hellenistic Civilization* (Western New England College.) Archived 2008-07-05 at the Wayback Machine.

[138] Marcinkowski, Christoph. *The Islamic World and the West.* 2009.

[139] McKay, John; Buckler, John; Wiesner-Hanks, Merry E; Hill, Bennett; and Clare Crowston. *History of Western Society Complete.* 2016.

[140] Eckstein, Arthur. *Rome Enters the Greek East.* 2012.

In the year 146 BCE, the Achaean League rebelled against its Roman allies for their annexation of political power and foreign policy in Greece.[141] The League lacked the military might to back up its rebellion, however. Romans came to Greece en masse that year and won a decisive victory against their detractors. It was thus that the power of the Mediterranean passed seamlessly from the ancient Hellenistic lands into those of the Roman Republic.

It has been falsely claimed that Greece underwent a cultural decline in the years prior to Roman occupation. This was not the case; it was merely by the point of the sword that the realm switched hands. There was no great dark age of Greece that heralded the coming of a new generation of conquerors, philosophers, and politicians; if anything, the dark age came with the Romans, not before. The Greeks were assimilated greedily by their captors, and all they achieved would soon appear to have been the achievements of Rome.

---

[141] Phang, Sara; Spence, Iain; and Douglas Kelly. *Conflict in Ancient Greece and Rome.* 2016.

Chapter 13 – From Greece to Rome

The appearance of the Roman Republic in the Greek world was, contextually speaking, quite unprecedented. After all, the Romans hadn't even existed for most of Athens' or Greece's lifespan. Though they arrived later from a Greek perspective, Rome had been in the making for at least a thousand years—and by the hand of a mythological Greek character, no less.

In the second millennium BCE, a Trojan man called Aeneas left the war-torn remains of his native city at the urging of the goddess Aphrodite—his mother—and his princely father. As a demi-god, he was protected by his powerful mother and was therefore one of the survivors of the ongoing wars with the Greeks. He fled by sea westward until coming upon the Italian shores. He climbed onto the land at the western side of the country and established his home there.[142]

Aeneas is credited with the creation of the Roman race, as his offspring and descendants were of mixed Trojan and native Italian heritage. His own son, Ascanius, built the ancient city of Alba Longa

---

[142] Virgil. *Aeneid.*

in which his own descendants, Romulus and Remus, were born many years later.[143] For centuries, Alba Longa was the largest and most influential city in all of Italy, but its time in the sun would not last. Soon, it would be Rome's turn to dazzle all of Western creation, piggybacking on the culture and success of the Hellenistic kingdoms and establishing itself as a great capital of Europe and the Mediterranean.

Romans taught their children that the great city had been founded by the demi-gods Romulus and Remus, who were twin brothers. The brothers had been condemned to death as infants because of a prophecy that said they would be responsible for the fall of their great-uncle, the King Amulius of Alba Longa. Amulius was willing to risk no chances on his power or his life, so he ordered his slaves to kill the babies. They took pity, however, and instead cast them down the Tiber River where they were found by a she-wolf. The wolf suckled the babies and cared for them in her cave until they were discovered by a shepherd called Faustulus.[144]

Faustulus and his wife cared for the brothers as their own children, and Romulus and Remus learned to tend sheep and take part in the rural politics of their adopted community. In young adulthood, they were swept up in a debate concerning the deposition of the ruling king of Alba Longa. Many citizens were in favor of Numitor—the boys' grandfather—over Amulius. Fighting ensued, and Remus was arrested and taken to Alba Longa. Romulus followed him there, and upon meeting the king, all was revealed about the true identities of the young sheepherders.[145]

Romulus and Remus did indeed live up to the prophecy, killing Amulius and installing their grandfather, Numitor, as king of Alba

---

[143] Ibid.

[144] Garcia, Brittany. "Romulus and Remus." *Ancient History Encyclopedia*. Ancient History Encyclopedia, 18 Apr 2018. Web. 21 Mar 2019.

[145] Ibid.

Longa. Then, eager for their own land to rule, they set out for the region of the seven hills and looked for the perfect place on which to establish their own grand city. Here, the brothers disagreed about how to proceed. Romulus set his sights on Palatine Hill, just above the very cave where they'd been nurtured by the wolf. Remus, however, preferred Aventine Hill. They could not come to a compromise, and so, they asked the gods for help in choosing a location. When both received signs they interpreted as positive, they still could not agree, and so, Romulus killed his brother and founded Rome on Palatine Hill.[146] He ruled there as its first king for 37 years before disappearing one day in a violent and mysterious storm.[147]

Like their not-too-distant neighbors, the Athenians, early Romans enjoyed the benefits of living on an easy trade route. Though not connected directly to the Mediterranean Sea, Rome was able to trade with other Italian communities and seafaring cultures of the Mediterranean thanks to its placement on the Tiber River. In those early years, the city's farmers and merchants imported marble, spices, and precious metals while exporting grains, wine, olives, and olive oil.[148] For middle-class workers and traders of the growing city, slaves were used to manage the import-export business of the day. Like the Greeks, Romans were dependent on slavery to keep building the city and its infrastructure, though unlike the Athenian slaves, Rome's were mostly foreigners who were captured outside the city-state.[149]

Rome grew steadily over the next several centuries, its kings amassing a decent amount of land in central Italy while fighting the Etruscans to the north and the Samnites and Greeks to the south.

[146] Ibid.

[147] Mavor, William Fordyce. *Universal History: Ancient and Modern.* 1804.

[148] Cartwright, Mark. "Trade in the Roman World." *Ancient History Encyclopedia.* Ancient History Encyclopedia, 12 Apr 2018. Web. 21 Mar 2019.

[149] Joshel, Sandra R. *Slavery in the Roman World.* 2010.

Certainly a force to be reckoned with in local terms, Rome was not particularly important or influential on the international scale until about the 3rd century BCE. Until then, Rome was a mere dot on the map of the known Western world next to the likes of Mesopotamia and the Persian Empire. Local trade and warfare were the focus of Rome's first kings, as was building a sound infrastructure.

Heavily influenced by the ideologies of the democratic cities of Greece, the Roman Kingdom did not last long. This period was characterized by factitious in-fighting and unrealistic financial management aimed at empire-building. Serious conflicts began in 579 BCE under the rule of the Etruscan-born Emperor Lucius Tarquinius Priscus. Priscus had taxed the Roman citizens more than they could stand to fund his endless military campaigns. He liked to show off his plunder and excess with parades in his own honor where he rode on a golden chariot dressed in a gold-embroidered toga. He sat on a special throne, held a scepter, and wore a royal purple garment as part of his outfit to celebrate his power as king and emperor.[150]

To his credit, Priscus poured a great deal of that plundered wealth back into Rome, finishing its outer fortifications and digging the Cloaca Maxima.[151] The Cloaca served as one of the ancient world's first sewage systems, by which the recently flooded outlying lands were drained and their excess routed to the Tiber. Priscus was probably responsible for the erection of the Circus Maximus as well, a massive stadium in which crowds would gather to watch chariot races and boxing matches.[152] Despite his attempts to strengthen Rome, Emperor Priscus was killed in a political coup in 579 BCE.[153]

---

[150] Florus. *The Epitome.*

[151] Hopkins, John North. *The Genesis of Roman Architecture.* 2016.

[152] Kenny, Peter Francis. *Monarchs.*

[153] Ibid.

In a political twist, Priscus' would-be usurpers were denied the throne in favor of Priscus' own son-in-law, Servius Tullius.[154] Following Tullius, it was either Priscus' son or grandson who would be the last king of Rome: Lucius Tarquinius Superbus. He was violent, relentless, and egotistical. He is said to have murdered family members—including his own king and father-in-law, Servius Tullius—to get to the throne of Rome.[155] Once he'd seized power, he continued the ongoing conquest of nearby city-states and small kingdoms and exhausted Rome's own resources by means of warfare and constant building projects. The citizens were already outraged with their king, and when the noblewoman Lucretia accused Superbus' son, Sextus, of rape, it was the final nail in the coffin of the Roman monarchy.[156]

Lucius Junius Brutus, already having gained the loyalty of the Roman army, joined their forces with the support of the local aristocracy and forced Superbus out of the city.[157, 158] Though the deposed king fought back multiple times with the allied help of the Etruscans, he never regained his city and died in exile in 495 BCE.[159] Brutus and Collatinus, the husband of Lucretia, were elected as Rome's first democratic consuls, and the Roman Republic was born.[160]

---

[154] Ibid.

[155] Titus Livius. *Ab urbe condita.*

[156] Matthes, Melisa M. *Rape of Lucretia and the Founding of Republics.* 2010.

[157] Stevenson, Tom. *Transformation of the Roman Republic.* 2014.

[158] Neill, Thomas Patrick. *A History of Western Civilization.* 1962.

[159] Eidinow, Esther. *The Oxford Companion to Classical Civilization.* 2014.

[160] Zoch, Paul A. *Ancient Rome: An Introductory History.* 2012.

Chapter 14 – The Roman Republic

Fundamentally, the government of the Roman Republic was organized according to three different political bodies: the Senate, the Assemblies, and the magistrates.[161] It was this multi-layered structure that gave the Republic its strength. With every stratum of the city's population engaged in some small part of governance, even an imperfect and aristocratically inclined system seemed infinitely more pleasing than the ultimate rule of a single dictator. Their motto was "Senatus Populusque Romanus," or "Senate and People of Rome."[162]

At the heart of the system was the famous Roman Senate, a body of men elected to discuss and enact the laws of the state. In place as an advisory board in the days of the Roman kings, the Senate had 300 members in 509 BCE.[163] It was in this administrative body that the roots of democracy—borrowed from the intellects of Greece—took an even firmer hold on Western civilization. Comprised of several hundred senators, officially clothed in the purple-striped toga and matching shoes of their office, the Senate's purpose was discussion

---

[161] Lintott, Andrew. *The Constitution of the Roman Republic.* 1999.

[162] Maesano, Luisa. *Ancient Rome Handbook.* 2017.

[163] Encyclopaedia Brittanica. "Senate Roman History." Web.

and legislation.[164] The men of the Senate met to discuss the issues, great and small, that faced their city-state and vote on how best to meet each challenge.

It was far from a perfectly fair system, but women's rights improved under its administration. Many women could divorce their husbands or conduct their own business, unlike their predecessors under the rule of the Roman kings.[165] There were essentially two classes of people in the Roman Republic: one was a small group of wealthy, landed aristocrats, known as the patricians, and the other was comprised of the non-noble workers, soldiers, small merchants, and the poor—the plebeians.[166]

The patricians were in charge of selecting and serving as the senators, thus exercising their aristocratic and democratic rights at the same time. As of the 5th century BCE, the plebeians were excluded from all parts of government and were expected to consult their patrician patriarch (a representative that each district possessed) to deal with any issues or legal grievances. Women, whether from the aristocracy or not, could neither be elected into the Senate nor place a vote.[167]

From within the Senate, two members were elected to hold the highest democratic office of consul.[168] It was important that there were two of these leaders so that they would have to agree with one another before enacting any laws or reforms. Additionally, one could stay in Rome and administer to the city while the second could oversee the work of the army as it endlessly marched into foreign territories collecting slaves, taxes, and valuables. Consuls were only

[164] Adkins, Lesley and Roy A. Adkins. *Handbook to Life in Ancient Rome.* 2014.

[165] Grubbs, Judith Evans. *Women and the Law in the Roman Empire.* 2002.

[166] Ibid.

[167] Ibid.

[168] Ibid.

allowed to serve one-year terms, a law set to restrain them from merely becoming new kings.[169]

Other magistrates beneath the consuls were the praetors, the quaestors, the aediles, and the other senators. Each of these roles was specifically defined. Praetors were responsible for attending to judgments in local courts; quaestors managed the city's finances and paid Rome's soldiers; plebeian aediles were a combination of city planners and civil servants, taking control of building projects and arranging public festivals; and finally, the Senate was in charge of delegating to the other groups and dealing with bigger issues like war.[170]

Under the rule of the kings, Roman plebeians had been unable to participate in the Senate, but they still made up the vast majority of the population of Rome and eventually used this to their advantage. In 494 BCE, they went on strike, demanding that their class be granted the right to represent itself in the Senate. To ensure that they were taken seriously, the strikers gathered together and walked out of Rome altogether, claiming that they would start a new city farther up the Tiber.[171] The Senate was forced to grant this demand as Rome's economy was largely based on the conquering and taxation of surrounding polities. The plebeians were granted the right to elect their own representatives, called tribunes, who argued on their behalf within the Senate and had the power to call a regular Plebeian Assembly. The assemblies were required so that tribunes could propose, discuss, and vote on laws that affected only non-patricians.

The Romans also had a fail-safe built into their government legislation that would be enacted in case the state was deprived of its consuls and the citizens were in imminent danger, say from an enemy army. In this case, the appointed magister populi, or dictator,

---

[169] Ibid.

[170] Ibid.

[171] Wells, H.G. *Outline of History.* 1951.

would step in, take total control such as that of an emperor, do whatever had to be done to protect the Roman Republic, and then hand power back to the Senate within six months.[172] The magister populi was ideally an experienced military general with the knowledge and strength necessary to lead Rome's soldiers to victory.

The Roman Republic spanned nearly five centuries, from the deposition of Lucius Tarquinius Superbus in 509 BCE to the introduction of the Roman Empire in 27 BCE.[173] During that timeframe, Rome not only gained international fame for its system of self-governance but also for its great feats of architecture, literature, higher learning, and military dominance. Not content to remain in the shadows of the Greeks, Babylonians, or Egyptians, the Romans set out to conquer the known world and bring their own culture—which they considered both unique and superior to all others—to the masses of uncultured hordes in Italy, the Mediterranean, Africa, Europe, and Asia.

---

[172] Wasson, Donald L. "Cincinnatus." *Ancient History Encyclopedia.* Ancient History Encyclopedia, 04 Apr 2017. Web. 22 Mar 2019.

[173] Adkins, Lesley and Roy A. Adkins. *Handbook to Life in Ancient Rome.* 2014.

Chapter 15 – The Borrowed Gods of Rome

If we refuse our homage to statues and frigid images, the very counterpart of their dead originals, with which hawks, and mice, and spiders are so well acquainted, does it not merit praise instead of penalty, that we have rejected what we have come to see is error? We cannot surely be made out to injure those whom we are certain are nonentities. What does not exist is in its nonexistence secure from suffering.

(Tertullian, *Apology*)

The Hellenic city-states had sprung up centuries before that of Rome, and Athens still stood as a beacon of philosophy, politics, and intellect to the people of Italy and the rest of the Mediterranean. In many ways, the culture that had been born in ancient Greece—particularly in Athens—simply stretched across the sea and planted itself in Rome. There, the philosophies of the great Greek thinkers took root, evolving slightly to accommodate their new home. Rome accepted these intangible gifts gratefully, always respectful of the great civilization that had come before it.

Due to the close relationship between Greece and Italy during their formative years on the same side of the Mediterranean, religious and spiritual ideas had flowed from one into the other. Particularly after the Macedonian Wars and the beginning of the Roman era, the shape of Rome's gods became much clearer. The Greek pantheon, including Zeus, Hera, Athena, and their brethren delighted the ears of the Italians and sparked their own spiritual imaginations. Hence, the gods and goddesses of the Romans were almost a carbon copy of those of the Greeks.[174] In place of Zeus, there was Jupiter, King of the Gods and himself the God of Thunder. For Poseidon, there was Neptune, God of the Sea. Even Cronus had a counterpart known as Saturn, father of Jupiter. More than a dozen Roman deities bear striking resemblances to those of the Greeks, and yet the new pantheon was granted full respect and faith from its citizens. Perhaps this was the fundamental philosophy of the Romans: to take what had been Greek and make it better, more personal.

After Rome had conquered and converted the greater part of Greece and the Mediterranean ring to its own empire, Roman aristocrats imported learned Greeks to teach their children.[175] In doing so, Roman citizens ensured the continuation of what they considered the best of Greek civilization. For their part, the enslaved Greek tutors of the Roman Republic made the most of their situation, teaching young Romans about the powerful and mystical gods and goddesses that had created the world and every creature on it. They taught numbers, the Greek alphabet, geometry, and advanced mathematics; they shared the philosophical writings of their own heroes and told stories written by Greeks from centuries past. It was a new day under a new empire, but the Greek civilization lived on, just as authoritative as it once had been, in the guise of the Roman Republic.

Just as the plethora of deities helped the Greeks make sense of themselves and the universe, so too did the Romans' pantheon.

---

[174] De la Bedoyere, Guy. *The Romans for Dummies.* 2011.

[175] Redmond, Marian. *Literacy and History: The Romans.* 2007.

Within Rome itself, the great Pantheon temple was built in the first part of the 2nd century CE to honor multiple gods and goddesses together in one place; its importance was such that it became a central feature of the city.[176]

In addition to the religious theft of the Greek gods, Romans seemed to pick and choose features of their faith and universe at will. The Egyptian cat goddess, Bastet, is a good example of this inclination. Worshiped as part of the Egyptians' own pantheon, Bastet was welcomed into many household altars within the Roman Empire.[177] It was one facet of life and religion that squarely differed between the Greeks and the Romans: the importance and symbolism of cats.

For Greeks, cats were really nothing special. Even though neighboring Egypt put its domestic and wild cats on literal pedestals, mummifying them alongside the bodies of dead pharaohs, the Greeks had no such affinity for the little felines.[178] Even the notion that a house cat could provide services by hunting mice, rats, and other pests was little help for its cause since Greek households had already employed domestic weasels for just that purpose.[179]

The Romans' relationship with the domestic cat was an entirely different story. From the first time domestic cats were introduced in Italy—probably by the Phoenicians—they were adored. [180] Immediately put to use alongside weasels for housekeeping duties, cats found themselves not only employed but celebrated members of Roman families. A pet cat was a common feature of the ancient

[176] Sullivan, George H. *Not Built in a Day: Exploring the Architecture of Rome.* 2009.

[177] Encyclopaedia Brittanica. "Bastet Egyptian Goddess." Mar 1 2019.

[178] Malek, Jaromir. *The Cat in Ancient Egypt.* 1997.

[179] Hard, Robin. *The Routledge Handbook of Greek Mythology.* 2003.

[180] Engels, Donald W. *Classical Cats: The Rise and Fall of the Sacred Cat.*

Roman home; even at the feet of their goddess of freedom, Libertas, a cat stood by.[181, 182]

The Roman gods and goddesses served their people as well as the Greek pantheon served its own believers. The ability to pick and choose their favorite pieces of culture, notably from Greece and Egypt, meant Romans could piece together what they believed was the best of all worlds. The fact that both Greek and Roman sets of deities survive in memory today shows the strength and pride both civilizations felt toward their own creations. To the modern onlooker, Rome's many deities may seem like Greek duplicates, but to a citizen of the ancient Mediterranean, it may have belied nothing more than the fact the era of Hellenistic kingdoms had officially given way to the Roman Republic.

---

[181] Adkins, Lesley and Roy A. Adkins. *Handbook to Life in Ancient Rome.* 2014.

[182] Elmes, James. *A General and Bibliographical Dictionary of the Fine Arts.* 1826.

Chapter 16 – The Classical Romans

Perhaps one of the most defining features of the Roman Republic was the belief of its own senators, tribunes, patricians, and plebeians that Rome was the quintessential form of human culture and civilization. But just what was it that set Romans apart from their neighbors near and far? Self-rule was certainly a large part of that image, but it wasn't democracy that Rome's legions brought to its conquered nations—it was a provincial dictatorship under a Roman magistrate.[183] Therefore, the apparent will of the Romans to impart their knowledge on everyone else equated fundamentally to egotism and Rome-centrism. Indeed, the belief of Rome in its innate correctness persists in Western culture to this day, in that the Romans are considered to have been the pinnacle of cultural enlightenment.

Nowhere was this culture better exemplified than in the city of Rome itself, which was home to perhaps one million people during this

---

[183] Encyclopaedia Brittanica. "Province Roman Government." Web.

period.[184] A strictly patriarchal society, Roman men ruled at home as well as in the Senate, holding legal ownership over their wives, daughters, and, even in some cases, the wives of their sons.[185] The men also held ownership of slaves who were usually purchased from traders who procured them during military raids in foreign lands. Sometimes, children were sold by parents who desperately needed money.[186] Slavery was not based on the color of one's skin or their national heritage but simply on their own misfortune at having been captured in the first place.

Slavery was rampant in Rome and was by no means confined to the household or the fields. Slaves learned any number of jobs and roles and performed these at the bidding of their masters. From sewage maintenance to accounting, any job could be held by a slave so long as his master wished it; as such, slaves were an integral part of the Roman economy and infrastructure, and without this huge source of labor, the city and Republic would not have been the same.[187]

Because of their diverse heritage, Roman slaves were often difficult to discern from a free man or woman. They wore the same tunics and togas of free plebeians and therefore blended within the society.[188] In the Senate, a law calling for all slaves to wear a specific uniform was debated heavily, but it was ultimately dismissed. Many senators believed that if the slaves could see how they outnumbered free men, it would cause a revolt.[189] There were, however, many incidents of slaves being legally freed by their masters, after which their children would be considered free citizens

[184] Stewart, David. *Inside Ancient Rome*. 2006.

[185] Grubbs, Judith Evans. *Women and the Law in the Roman Empire*. 2002.

[186] Ibid.

[187] Hunt, Peter. *Ancient Greek and Roman Slavery*. 2017.

[188] Gardner, Jane, and Thomas Weidemann. *Representing the Body of the Slave*. 2013.

[189] Ibid.

of the Republic, able even to serve in the Senate (in the case of males).[190] Though freemen could not run for office, they could vote and hold some government jobs.[191]

City life was mostly centered on the Forum and the central business district. Citizens could shop for clothing, textiles, spices, fresh and preserved foods, meat and fish, fruits, vegetables, and luxury items like shoes and books. Most people went to the market at the Forum, but patricians often shopped in specialty stores where they could buy meat, home furnishings, and slaves.[192] Poor Romans and slave families usually shopped in a different market that sold mostly vegetables, millet bread, and lentils, the most affordable foods.[193, 194] In the central business district, one could find banks, barbershops, and other professional services necessary for daily life. Interspersed between shops, marketplaces, commercial buildings, and other edifices were the auctioneers and street vendors, pushing their wares here and there along the cobbled streets between crowds of pedestrians and aristocrats carried on canopied couches.

The building and city planning skills of the ancient Romans must have been a marvel to behold in action. The architects and laborers of the city weren't just there to build walls and dig drainage ditches; they intended to revolutionize urban wastewater management altogether. The man behind the brand-new technology was Appius Claudius Caecus.[195] Appius designed and built Rome's very first aqueduct, the Aqua Appia, in 312 BCE, and it was so effective that

---

[190] McGeough, Kevin M. *The Romans: New Perspectives.* 2004.

[191] Ibid.

[192] Holleran, Claire. *Shopping in Ancient Rome.*

[193] Ibid.

[194] Carr, K.E. Roman food – rich and poor. Quatr.us Study Guides, September 1, 2017. Web. March 22, 2019.

[195] Bunsun, Matthew. *Encyclopedia of the Roman Empire.* 2014.

the realm built another ten of them over the course of the next century.[196]

The premise of the new sewage system was simple, as it was based on gravity pulling fresh water from its source through pipes and tunnels to wherever the architects wanted it to go. Putting that idea into concrete, stone, and brick, however, took an incredible amount of forethought and even more hard labor. Once the designs had been laid out to bring fresh water into the city and siphon away wastewater, the great work of building remained to be done.

The invention of Roman concrete was essential to the contemporary architecture of the Roman Republic, especially for the aqueducts. Instead of quarry rocks or flimsy mud bricks, concrete was a wet mix of small rocks, ceramic, and other building debris with gypsum, quicklime, and pozzolana.[197] Pozzolana is a type of volcanic ash found throughout Rome and especially in the region of Campania, as it surrounds Mount Vesuvius. Thanks to the special properties of pozzolana, the concrete hardened into a durable brick or filler that would withstand cracking even better than modern cement. It also set while damp, which gave builders the opportunity to work in the rain and even underwater.[198]

Seawater reacted with the concrete perfectly to create a fixed, durable structure that outlasted any other type of contemporary construction.[199] Builders used these cement bricks as the foundation of their aqueduct bridges and tunnels, then layered on clay bricks for further strength and support.[200] It was with simple cement and brick that Appius' teams transformed Rome and its countryside into a land of giant, double-arched bridge-ways, some of which are still standing and in use

---

[196] Encyclopaedia Brittanica. "Aqueduct Engineering." Web.

[197] Adkins, Lesley and Roy A. Adkins. *Handbook to Life in Ancient Rome.* 2014.

[198] Jackson, Marie D; Mulcahy, Sean R; Chen, Heng; Li, Yao; Li, Qinfei; Cappelletti, Piergiulio; and Hans-Rudolf Wenk. "Phillipsite and Al-tobermorite mineral cements produced through low-temperature water-rock reactions in Roman marine concrete." July 01, 2017.
[199] Ibid.

[200] Aicher, Peter J. *Guide to the Aqueducts of Ancient Rome.* 1995.

today. One of these ancient structures, known as the Aqua Virgo, feeds the 18th-century Trevi Fountain in Rome.[201]

While the aqueducts flowed and the bridges held fast, trade and business were the daily focus of Rome's patriarchs. For wealthy children, however, it was school. Rome's informal educational system was meant to teach young children grammar and basic numbers. From the age of about six, both girls and boys of wealthy families attended lessons that taught them how to count, write, and read.[202] When those students reached the age of twelve, the boys continued on, learning Greek, Latin, literature, and public speaking. At that point, the vast majority of girls was excluded from further education, though a rare few were allowed to continue on in their lessons. Normally, noble girls were married off after the age of twelve, which took precedence over schooling.[203]

It was a system heavily borrowed from that of the ancient Greeks, from whom the Romans took a great many pieces of culture. In deference to the empire that had come before, Rome's tutors and aristocrats put a great deal of emphasis on learning Greek letters and classical poetry from authors of previous centuries. The works of Homer and Hesiod, some of the earliest Greek poets, were frequently used in private and public classrooms for students to read and memorize.

Schooling was neither mandatory nor state funded by the Roman Republic, but it was nevertheless a cornerstone of their national identity.[204, 205] Public classes, considered more affordable to the non-

---

[201] Roda, Isabel. "Aqueducts: Quenching Rome's Thirst." National Geographic *History Magazine*. November/December 2016.

[202] Rawson, Beryl. *Children and Childhood in Roman Italy.* 2003.

[203] C N Trueman "Roman Education" historylearningsite.co.uk. The History Learning Site, 16 Mar 2015. 5 Mar 2019.

[204] Oxford Classical Dictionary, Third Edition. 1996.

[205] Morgan, Teresa. "Assessment in Roman Education." *Assessment in Education, Vol. 8, No.1.* March 2001.

wealthy, lacked structure in terms of hours of attendance or knowledge tests; however, oral reports, question-and-answer sessions, and presentations were commonly used to determine the extent of students' knowledge.[206]

Despite the commonplace employment of tutors, households were often also taught at the knee of their patriarch.[207] Considered the most intelligent member of the family, fathers wanted to be the one to impart knowledge onto their children and in so doing claim the praise rewarded them for good intellect. Teenagers who were compelled toward higher education were most likely to travel to Greece for lessons in philosophy, mathematics, and astronomy.[208] Even in the centuries following the decline of the Greek civilization, the best philosophers were considered to be found only in Athens.

Within the Republic, fully-educated men went on to become architects, senators, and generals.[209] Each of these careers was an integral pillar to Roman culture: architects put their mark in solid stone and beautiful, shining marble; senators attested to the greatness of the Republic and its democratic system; and generals kept the army fit, sharp, and at the ready to strike or defend as needed. Between them, they made the most lasting features and impressions of the Roman Republic: the arches, domes, and concrete structures that would last a millennium; the forums whose lectures influenced entire civilizations; and a territory that nearly entirely encapsulated the Mediterranean Sea.

---

[206] Bonner, Stanley. *Education in Ancient Rome.* 2012.

[207] Ibid.

[208] Encyclopaedia Brittanica. "Roman Adoption of Hellenistic Education." Web.

[209] Michael Chiappetta, "Historiography and Roman Education," *History of Education Journal* 4, no. 4 1953.

Chapter 17 – The Gladiators

The bloody wound

Of the gladiator

Gurgles out life's end.

The cries of acclimations from the stands

Fill the sky with raging tigers.

Waving their arms about to incite the masses

The aging notables add an air of dignity to the arena.

Making their separate entries

they KNEEL

over the still-warm corpses

Of the young. Their withered lips they pose

Upon the fresh flowing wounds

And, to prolong their lives – so they believe,

Suck, ravenously suck out the blood, blood, blood.

Fresh blood from the sun

Flowing into filthy veins

As into sewage pipes,

And thus the Heart of the Nation is abandoned.

(Visar Zhiti)[210]

Gladiatorial entertainment demonstrated a violent and bloody part of the Roman psyche, one that contrasted sharply with the citizens' vision of themselves as the pinnacle of sophistication and intelligence. Though the members of the republic, as well as the later empire, enjoyed attending theatrical performances, watching dancers, and listening to the compositions of talented musicians, it was the gladiator competitions that really pulled in the crowds. The massive Colosseum was completed in 80 CE for the primary purpose of serving Rome's unquenchable thirst for blood and showmanship.[211] Able to hold 50,000 audience members, the Colosseum was the most sophisticated theater in the ancient world.[212]

Playwrights used the massive theater to recreate famous battles and mythological stories of the gods, public executions were carried out there in full view of the clamoring public, and in the early days of the new Colosseum, the floor was flooded for impressive reenactments of sea battles.[213] Underground, a complex series of tunnels and chambers were constructed to house slaves and an array of animals that were used in the performances.[214] The slaves, captured from all corners of the Roman Empire, were forced into

---

[210] Zhiti, Visar. Translation by Robert Elsie. "The Condemned Apple: Selected Poetry." 2004.

[211] Kleiner, Fred S. *Gardner's Art Through the Ages: A Global History.* 2009.

[212] Ibid.

[213] Hopkins, Keith, and Mary Beard. *The Colosseum.* 2005.

[214] Ibid.

hand-to-hand combat, first in training and then on the grand stage. These slaves did not always necessarily fight to the death, but eventually, they would most likely meet their end by the sword. New recruits learned the right combat tactics over time, and some even held their own against opponent after opponent in the arena, gaining the respect and adoration of the city.

Various classes of gladiators battled in Rome's arenas. Based on a fighter's experience and rank among the other gladiators, he might have been a thraex or murmillo—that is, a foot soldier armed with a shield and sword and fitted with armor,[215] or a fighter lacking most body armor but sporting a finned helmet, a three-foot shield, and a gladius.[216] He might also have been an eques, the sort of fighter who entered the arena on horseback, or an essedarius, who fought from a chariot. The murmillo fights were the most popular with audiences, but there was a great deal of variety available for the gladiatorial aficionado. Some men were set up to fight lions, wolves, and other animals, while some fought one another with nothing more than a trident and a net. Christians were famously thrown in against lions without anything to defend themselves with.[217]

Though most of the fighters were men, women also fought in the arenas during the 1st and 2nd centuries CE, until they were banned from entering by Emperor Septimius Severus.[218] Until 200 CE, they suffered alongside their male slave counterparts but were often sent in merely to make the patriarchal audience members laugh at their supposed inadequacies in battle. It was not unusual for female

---

[215] Ibid.

[216] Nossov, Konstantin. *Gladiator: The Complete Guide to Ancient Rome's Bloody Fighters.* 2011.

[217] Hopkins, Keith, and Mary Beard. *The Colosseum.* 2005.

[218] Abrams, Robert B. *The Colosseum: A History.* 2017.

fighters to find themselves pitted against male dwarves, though usually, they fought one another.[219]

In every batch of new fighters, one might be destined for fame. One such gladiator was Spartacus, a rebellious slave from the southeastern European region of Thrace.[220] Having possibly served in a section of the Roman army, Spartacus was for some reason stripped of his rank and made a slave under the foot of aristocratic Rome.[221] Eventually, he was sold and taken to Lentulus Batiatus, the owner of the realm's largest gladiatorial training grounds near the city of Capua.[222] Alongside the other men, Spartacus was forced to take an oath that he would follow orders or risk corporal punishment. That probably didn't seem to matter much to the groups of men who regularly marched into Capua to fill the space left by the uncountable dead fighters. One way or another, they were doomed to die at the hands of the trainers or each other.

Although the men probably bunked together in dark, tiny rooms underground, they were not inclined to befriend one another. There were various reasons they kept themselves emotionally distant; the first was simply a mixture of languages that made communication among the recruits quite difficult. Secondly, the men knew that when they were put into the arena to kill each other, they couldn't face taking down a friend. It was better to follow the rules and stay alive by slaughtering strangers.

Spartacus thought differently. He dared to pit himself against the powers that be and rallied his fellow slaves to rise up against their masters in force. Spartacus enacted one of the most memorable escapes in Roman history. Together with a small force of at least

---

[219] Hubbard, Ben. *Gladiators*. 2016.

[220] Castleden, Rodney. *Conflicts that Changed the World*. 2008.

[221] Ibid.

[222] Ibid.

seventy gladiators, Spartacus and his men plundered the Capua camp's kitchen for knives before fighting their way ruthlessly out of the training center and into the streets, where they commandeered several wagons loaded with armor and weapons.[223] The men plundered Capua and recruited many more slaves before retreating into relative safety on Mount Vesuvius where they regrouped and made further plans.

The gladiators' rebellion sparked the Third Servile War of the Roman Republic.[224] It was the last of the great slave rebellions against the powerful republic and perhaps the most shocking. Spartacus and most of his companions weren't content merely to slink away to find their own personal freedom, especially after Roman soldiers pursued them to Mount Vesuvius and laid siege to the volcano. Not ready to give up, the gladiators crafted ropes from vines atop the mountain and climbed stealthily down the opposite side, attacking the soldiers' camp before retreating once more. In the next attack, the rebels managed not only to vanquish the soldiers but to arm themselves with the very weapons meant to end the rebellion.

Excited by the great success of the slave army, tens of thousands of Rome's bonded laborers fled the homes of their masters and joined the ranks of the gladiator army. Spartacus, Crixus, and Oenomaus became the party's leaders, who together led some 40,000 slaves and other recruits to fight their way out of Italy.[225] The group then split, with some heading northwest to cross the Alps and the rest intending to return to Thrace. Though the former slaves had proved themselves capable of dodging attacks and potentially finding their way to safety, Spartacus' group of mostly Thracian slaves had second thoughts about abandoning the powerful army they'd formed. The

---

[223] Ibid.

[224] Kohn, George Childs. *Dictionary of Wars.* 2013.

[225] Ibid.

army no longer answered to the whims of Spartacus and decided amongst themselves to use its strength to pillage the country.

In his biography of Crassus, Plutarch wrote of Spartacus' movements during the Third Servile War:

> ...he marched his army towards the Alps, intending, when he had passed them, that every man should go to his own home, some to Thrace, some to Gaul. But they, grown confident in their numbers, and puffed by with their success, would give no obedience to him, but went about and ravaged Italy; so that now the senate was not only moved at the indignity and baseness, both of the enemy and of the insurrection, but, looking upon it as a matter of alarm and dangerous consequence.[226]

Bolstered by their continued success, the slave army considered the brash tactic of sacking Rome itself, but eventually, logic dictated that they remain out of the capital. Instead, they moved into the south of Italy. While the rebellious force considered its next move, Rome's consuls sent Marcus Crassus to crush the rebellion. All throughout 71 CE, Crassus' 40,000 soldiers chased Spartacus and his followers across Italy, until finally, with the help of Pompey the Great's army returning from Hispania, the rebels were captured and slaughtered.[227]

> [Spartacus,] pushing his way towards Crassus himself through many flying weapons and wounded men, he did not indeed reach him, but slew two centurions who fell upon him together. Finally, after his companions had taken to flight, he stood alone, surrounded by his foes, and was still defending himself when he was cut down.[228]

---

[226] Plutarch. *Lives of the Noble Greeks and Romans.*

[227] Kohn, George Childs. *Dictionary of Wars.* 2013.

[228] Plutarch. *Plutarch's Lives.*

Some 6,000 surviving slaves were crucified along the road back to Rome while others were thrown back into the gladiator camps.[229] Though the defeat of the slaves seems crushingly thorough, some contemporaries and historians like to speculate that Spartacus himself managed to escape once more.

The last recorded gladiatorial competition in Rome was in the year 404 CE when they were banned by Emperor Honorius.[230]

---

[229] Ibid.

[230] Hanel, Rachael. *Gladiators.* 2007.

Chapter 18 – Julius Caesar, Part 1

Gaius Julius Caesar, more commonly known by his cognomen Julius Caesar, traced his lineage back to a prince of Troy who was celebrated as the son of the goddess Venus.[231] With nothing less than the blood of the gods running through his veins, there could be little wonder that such a man would become one of the greatest heroes of Rome. He was born into the aristocracy in 100 BCE after a difficult delivery that is believed to be the first recorded case of the appropriately named caesarean section.[232] His father, also named Gaius Julius Caesar, had been Praetor Magistrate of the Province of Asia, and like the elder Caesar, the younger excelled in politics.

As a patrician, young Julius was expected to serve a term in the Senate and in the army; he did so and performed well in both roles. When he was about fifteen, however, his father's death made him the head of the household and inspired him to take a different career

---

[231] Lovano, Michael. *All Things Julius Caesar.* 2014.

[232] Stevenson, Tom. *Julius Caesar and the Transformation of the Roman Republic.* 2014. Note: Historians do not agree on the technical details of this difficult birth. Even if this was the unlikely first case of an infant being cut from its mother's body while the mother survived, the method had been used before Caesar's time to rescue unborn children from the womb of a deceased mother.

path.[233] Knowing that he needed financial security more than anything else, Caesar turned to the priesthood. Religion was serious business in a city where rulers claimed sacred, holy ancestry from Zeus and Poseidon themselves, and joining the priesthood meant that a man's family could enjoy the respect of their fellow citizens and enough money to live comfortably. There was one problem, unfortunately: the girl who Julius had already promised to marry was not from an aristocratic family. Priests were required to marry patrician women, so Caesar ended the engagement and married a patrician girl named Cornelia Cinna.[234, 235]

His plan backfired hideously as the city's ongoing political debates had reached a breaking point between the two main factions, the Populares and Optimates. The first ideology posited that the best way to govern Rome was through democratic principles and the mobilization of the lower classes.[236] However, many Romans were of the opinion that the Optimate platform was best, in which the aristocracy held supreme power over the plebeians because they were intellectually superior.[237] Julius and his family subscribed to the Populares ideology.[238]

The Cinnas were politically allied with Caesar's uncle, Gaius Marius. Cinna was a consul of Rome at the time of his daughter's wedding to Caesar, and his influence helped the latter become the High Priest of Jupiter.[239, 240] Soon afterward, however, the Optimate

---

[233] Dugan, Christine. *Julius Caesar: Roman Leader.* 2007.

[234] Mark, Joshua J. "Julius Caesar." *Ancient History Encyclopedia.* Web. 28 April 2011.

[235] Lovano, Michael. *All Things Julius Caesar.* 2014.

[236] Ibid.

[237] Ibid.

[238] Ibid.

[239] Colegrove, Michael and Micha Colegrove, Phd. *Distant Voices: Listening to the Leadership Lessons of the Past.* 2007.

enemy of Marius and Cinna, Lucius Cornelius Sulla Felix, marched on Rome as the army's general and seized power. Once Sulla had installed himself as the dictator of Rome in 81 BCE, he rid the city of his enemy Populares, and Caesar was stripped of his priesthood and instructed to divorce his wife.[241, 242] Refusing, the married couple left their home in exile. They were able to return thanks to the diplomatic outreach of his maternal family, but he was ultimately unable to pursue his career as High Priest of Jupiter.

There was one other way that Caesar knew how to earn a living, and that was in the army. It was not an easy job, but the work of a soldier kept Julius out of Rome and away from the man who had rebelled against his uncle and turned the Republic back into a dictatorship. He didn't return until Sulla's death in 78 BCE when he felt it was safe to walk along the streets of Rome without danger of attack from the dictator's allies.[243] Unfortunately, Caesar's wealth had long since been confiscated by Sulla as punishment for refusing to divorce Cornelia.[244] It was only in a lower-class part of the city that the newly returned exiles could afford housing, but he took it up all the same.

Those first years of his return to Roman life saw Julius Caesar take up public speaking, a habit he became well known for. Politics were his chosen theme, and Caesar spent hours speaking to groups about what he viewed as the disgraceful behavior of several of Rome's former governors. Through these regular monologues, Caesar's

[240] Yenne, Bill. *Julius Caesar: Lessons in Leadership from the Great Conqueror.* 2012.

[241] McKenzie, Richard. *Ancient Chronologies the Roman Republic.* 2008.

[242] Mark, Joshua J. *"Julius Caesar Definition."* *Ancient History Encyclopedia.* 28 April 2011.

[243] Crawford, Michael Hewson. *The Roman Republic.* 1993.

[244] Adam Alexander. *Classical Biography.* 1800.

personal characteristics—specifically his high-pitched voice and erratic hand gestures—came to exemplify him.

During a trip across the sea, possibly en route to study public speaking under the famed Apollonius Molon, Caesar was taken hostage by pirates and held prisoner on a tiny Greek island. During his 38-day imprisonment, Caesar took it upon himself to practice public speaking with his captors, who were apparently very much entertained by his flapping arms, squeaky voice, and obvious superiority complex.[245] When the man's captors told him they demanded twenty talents of silver to release him, he confidently offered to pay fifty instead.[246] The deal was done. When Julius was released, he returned to Rome, raised an army, and then captured and killed the pirates who'd kept him hostage.[247] After that, he pursued law and politics.

Over the next decade, Caesar moved up Rome's political ranks. He began as the military tribune, a position in which he was responsible for representing the army to the Senate, and was eventually granted the governorship of the province of Spain.[248] In 60 BCE, Caesar had become powerful and liked enough to form a political alliance with two other ambitious politicians: Marcus Licinius Crassus and Pompey the Great. This union would be called the First Triumvirate.[249] The purpose of the triumvirate was to put the right pressure on the Senate to ensure it passed several bills that were in Caesar's, Crassus', and Pompey's best interests. Ultimately, they wanted to secure the consulship of Rome for themselves, and this

---

[245] Plutarch. *The Parallel Lives.*

[246] Mark, Joshua J. "Julius Caesar Definition." *Ancient History Encyclopedia.* 28 April 2011.

[247] Ibid.

[248] Ibid.

[249] Ibid.

came to fruition the very next year when Julius Caesar was elected as consul.[250]

The first bill Caesar introduced to the Senate was cleverly designed to earn him the love of the people of the Roman Republic while leaving him untouchable by irritated senators. His plan was to give free land to the poor farmers and veterans of the Republic who owned nothing for themselves.[251] It was a two-prong plan in which the poor of the Republic would be so grateful that they would become irrevocably loyal to their consul; secondly, it was meant to portray Caesar as selflessly infallible within the Senate. It worked but not at all the way the consul had intended. Senators disagreed heartily with splitting up public and private landholdings, and they walked out of the meeting when their new consul forcefully ejected an opponent from the Senate building.[252] Caesar thumbed his nose at the senators and took the case directly to the plebeian assembly, who were convinced to support him alongside Crassus and Pompey.[253] Thanks to the additional pressure of the plebeians and Rome's most powerful citizens, the Senate eventually voted to pass the bill.

He'd lost the support of Rome's conservative senators but gained the love of the poor, who far outnumbered the aristocracy.

[250] Encyclopaedia Brittanica. "Julius Caesar Roman Ruler." Web. Feb 13 2019.

[251] Campbell, Phillip. *The Story of Civilization: VOLUME I.* 2016.

[252] Dio, Cassius. *Roman History* 38.3.

[253] Encyclopaedia Brittanica. "Julius Caesar Roman Ruler." Web. Feb 13 2019.

Chapter 19 – Julius Caesar, Part 2

One of Caesar's main objectives in obtaining the consulship of Rome was the governorship of Gaul. It was common practice for consuls to be given personal responsibility over one Roman province, and he wanted to make sure that province was the most potentially lucrative of the Republic. Gaul, a Celtic civilization centered in modern France, had formerly been so extensive that it stretched from Celtic Britain to northern Italy. Subjugated under the force of the Roman Republic in its lower regions, its native culture and language dwindled. Julius Caesar knew very well that the lands beyond Roman Gaul's borders were filled with resources ripe for the taking, and he would let nothing get in his way. He envisioned all the splintered territories of Gaul, from Celtic Britain to Italy, under his control.

Caesar, greatly in debt thanks to expansive campaigning, was thrilled to be appointed the governor of Cisalpine Gaul in 58 BCE.[254] When the governor of the twin state Transalpine Gaul died that year, his administrative land was transferred to Caesar as well.[255] The

---

[254] Gilliver, Kate. *Caesar's Gallic Wars: 58-50 BC.*

[255] Ibid.

consul took on these responsibilities with gusto, immediately organizing counter-measures to stop Helvetii migrants—a Celtic tribe who actively sought new lands to settle at the tip of their swords—from crossing through his provinces. His first move was to construct a massive wall along the eastern side of the Rhone River, 29 kilometers (19 miles) in length.[256] Well aware that he was not permitted to take Gaul's armies out of Roman land without the express permission of the Senate, Caesar used the Helvetians as an excuse to do just that.

Caesar's forces slaughtered the armed migrants, pushing them decisively out of reach of the new wall and Roman borders. Caesar sent word home that he expected further pushback from the enemy, and he demanded the freedom to do as he liked with the army. The request was not well received at home, where many senators believed Caesar to be inventing problems and wasting resources for the sake of his own glory. The consul's detractors went so far as to appeal to Pompey the Great, telling him that if such behavior were to continue, Julius Caesar would replace Pompey as the city's most influential character. It was too late to make such claims, however, since Pompey had fallen in love with none other than the daughter of his political ally-cum-rival, Julia Caesar, and married her at the behest of Julius himself.[257]

Far from Rome, Julius Caesar was isolated from the arguments of the Senate but ultimately found himself granted the power to take Gaul's army wherever he deemed necessary. The Senate agreed to do so only on the basis that it must be necessary to protect Rome's provinces, which they were convinced of thanks to his lengthy letters home describing his exploits on the battlefield.[258] In truth, Caesar intended to do much more than simply defend his borders.

---

[256] Freeman, Philip. *Julius Caesar.* 2008

[257] Ibid.

[258] Gwynn, David M. *The Roman Republic: A Very Short Introduction.* 2012.

Determined to conquer whomever he saw fit despite his consulship having ended, Caesar set his sights on the Germanic war-leader, Ariovistus, who had dared to attack the Roman-allied people of Aedui.[259]

Ariovistus and his people, like virtually all cultures that lay to the north of the Roman Republic, were considered barbarians by Caesar and his contemporaries. They worshiped different gods and consulted oracles that were strange to the Romans, and therefore, they were believed to be inferior to the Republic in all ways.[260] Caring very little for the traditions and beliefs of his opponents, Caesar took advantage of the news that Ariovistus had been told by his gods not to fight until the new moon.[261] Roman forces rode up to the enemy encampment and prepared to fight anyway, forcing Ariovistus' men to defend themselves. Julius Caesar knew that the Germans believed themselves to be defying their gods, and this was exactly the negative mindset he wanted to exploit. The battle ended victoriously for the Romans and left Ariovistus' lands in the hands of Caesar.[262] Triumphantly, the consul pressed onward until he'd annexed modern France and Belgium for himself and Rome.

Rome's Senate became divided on the subject of Caesar's Gallic Wars. Though Crassus and Pompey continued to support their ally, a faction of senators believed that Caesar's actions were that of a king and would-be dictator, not a governor or a general of the army. Above all, the Senate was meant to protect the democratic system and not individuals with such expensive ambitions. Elections were held in 55 BCE, during which Crassus soothed the concerned senators and was appointed consul with Pompey.[263] In addition,

---

[259] Caesar, Julius. *Commentaries on the Gallic War*

[260] Mark, Joshua J. "The Goths." *Ancient History Encyclopedia.* 12 October 2014.

[261] Freeman, Philip. *Julius Caesar.* 2008.

[262] Caesar, Julius. *Commentaries on the Gallic War*

[263] Ibid.

Pompey was appointed Governor of Spain, Caesar was awarded another five years in Gaul, and Crassus was made Governor of Syria. [264, 265] Immediately, Crassus set out for the frontier of Syria, intent on pushing his borders just as Caesar was doing in Gaul.

In Rome, during 54 BCE, Caesar's daughter Julia died during the difficult delivery of Pompey's baby.[266] The baby died a few days later, leaving the widowed and bereaved Pompey devastated. With no more personal ties to his political ally, Pompey withdrew his support for Caesar, formally ending the triumvirate. Beyond a loss of brotherhood, Pompey and Caesar became bitter rivals. The next year was even more difficult for Caesar when his last ally, Crassus, died in a disastrous military campaign against Parthia.[267] The triumvirate was finished, and Julius Caesar was on his own where politics were concerned.

By 52 BCE, Rome had divided itself in two, half rioting for Pompey the Great—the only appointed consul that year—and half for the conquering leader, Julius Caesar.[268] Gangs dominated the streets, rampaging, beating, and burning. The Senate building went up in flames.[269] In Gaul, things were no better, as a Gallic ruler by the name Vercingetorix rallied his people in Gaul to fight against the occupying Roman troops.[270] The Gallic forces of Vercingetorix burned the farmland and food stores of the Roman army, intent on

[264] Ibid.

[265] Paterculis, Velleius: *The Roman History.* 2011.

[266] William Smith (editor.) *A New Classical Dictionary of Greek and Roman Biography, Mythology and Geography.* 1851.

[267] Caesar, Julius. *Commentaries on the Gallic War.*

[268] Colegrove, Michael and Micha Colegrove, Phd. *Distant Voices: Listening to the Leadership Lessons of the Past.* 2007.

[269] Lendering, Jona. Translated by S.J. Leinbach. *Stad in marmer.* 2002.

[270] Rollin, Charles, and Jean Baptise L. Crevier. *The Roman History.* 1768.

starving them out of Gaul altogether. Caesar found Vercingetorix's huge Gallic army between him and his own legions wintering in northern Gaul. He had to bypass Vercingetorix's army by making a difficult journey over the snow-covered mountains in the dead of winter with only a handful of troops. From there, he traveled until he reached modern-day Dijon, France. Within days, Caesar assembled his entire Gallic army and was ready to attack.

Warfare in Gaul calmed by the following year as Caesar's forces prevailed against those of the unified Gauls, but serious political rivalry had begun between Caesar's and Pompey's supporters in Rome.[271] Pompey had been appointed as Rome's single consul, and with the support of most of the Senate, he instructed Caesar to return to Rome alone and give up his governorship.[272] The great military general was faced with a serious problem. Should he follow orders and face the wrath of the Senate or capitalize on the social unrest in the city and take the opportunity to claim himself as dictator? If he took his army and crossed that border, marked by the Rubicon River, back into Roman territory, it would immediately signal civil war.

With his army behind him, Caesar chose to cross the Rubicon.

---

[271] Caesar, Julius. *Commentaries on the Gallic War.*

[272] Redonet, Fernando Lillo. "How Julius Caesar Started a Big War by Crossing a Small Stream." National Geographic *History Magazine.* March/April 2017.

Chapter 20 – The Roman Empire

Friends, Romans, countrymen, lend me your ears;

I come to bury Caesar, not to praise him;

The evil that men do lives after them,

The good is oft interred with their bones,

So let it be with Caesar...

(Marc Antony in William Shakespeare's *Julius Caesar*)

As Caesar's forces advanced southward, Pompey directed his own army out of Rome and into Greece, leaving his Spanish lands exposed. Caesar fought Pompey's remaining forces in Spain first, conquering them as their leader waited for his rival in Greece. The next year, they met at the Battle of Pharsalus in Greece, and Caesar's army gained a decisive victory.[273] Afterward, Pompey fled to Egypt looking for sanctuary and was assassinated for the attempt.[274]

---

[273] Ibid.

[274] Ibid.

At the time, Egypt was in a similar state of civil war as were the powers of Rome, and Caesar saw a way to make the most of this situation. Making haste to Egypt in pursuit of his ex-ally, Caesar was presented the head of Pompey by a tutor of co-Pharaoh Ptolemy XIII. According to Plutarch, Caesar wept at the sight and made to protect the head until he could arrange a proper burial. Whether he was truly angry about the murder of his old friend is unknown, but in any case, he turned to the matter of the feuding co-rulers of Egypt: Ptolemy XIII and his sister-bride, Cleopatra VII.

In a bid to sway the powerful diplomat to her own cause, Queen Cleopatra visited Caesar alone in his quarters by surprise. Plutarch wrote that the queen had herself wrapped up in a rug and was delivered to Caesar, fearful of being seen by guards and enemies. The two became fast friends and lovers, and after peace-making tactics between the two Egyptian leaders failed, Caesar agreed to fight at Cleopatra's side against Ptolemy.[275]

The cultural significance of Ptolemy and the Egyptian Kingdom was not lost on Julius Caesar. He visited the tomb of Alexander the Great and pondered his own means of making a lasting legacy in a country that was more ancient than either of their realms had ever been.[276] Ultimately, though he was not naturally inclined to support the murder of any members of the Ptolemaic Dynasty, Caesar accepted the fact that an alliance with Cleopatra may signify the end for Pharaoh Ptolemy XIII. Indeed, the brother of his beloved Egyptian queen drowned in the river Nile after his defeat by the combined forces of his sister and the Roman general in 47 BCE.[277]

That same year, Caesar's powerful general, Marc Antony, convinced the Senate to make Caesar dictator.[278] The Senate agreed to such a

---

[275] History. "Cleopatra commits suicide." Web. Updated February 25, 2019.

[276] Saunders, Nicolas J. *Alexander's Tomb: The Two-Thousand Year Obsession.* 2007.

[277] Grant, Michael. *Cleopatra: Cleopatra.* 2011.

[278] Patricia, Southern. *Mark Antony: A Life.* 2010.

condition only due to the fact that they wanted their consul to conclude his political dealings in Egypt and find a solution within that time. He complied and supported Cleopatra in marrying her 12-year-old brother Ptolemy XIV to consolidate the authority of the Egyptian queen with a necessary male counterpart.[279] The marriage was in law only; Cleopatra was the willing consort of Julius Caesar and by that time was probably pregnant with his child.

As soon as he was certain that Cleopatra's throne was secure, Caesar left Egypt for Rome. His temporary dictatorship had been extended in perpetuity, which infuriated members of the Senate; these irate senators took it upon themselves to ensure their realm remained democratic.[280] On March 15, 44 BCE, more than 60 conspiring senators accosted Julius Caesar outside the Theatre of Pompey, many of them stabbing him to death.[281]

Marc Antony and two of Caesar's most trusted allies organized to form the Second Triumvirate, after which they killed their friend's murderers and claimed leadership of the empire.[282] It was a fragile alliance, particularly given Antony's ongoing affair with Queen Cleopatra in Egypt. To smooth things over with Octavius, a fellow triumvirate member and Caesar's adopted son, Antony, married the former's sister Octavia.[283] It was of little use, however, since Cleopatra continued to bear his children. In 32 BCE, the Senate declared war on Egypt and deemed Marc Antony as a traitor to Rome.[284] Antony and Cleopatra fought back against Octavius' forces

---

[279] Ibid.

[280] Wasson, Donald L. "The Murder of Julius Caesar." *Ancient History Encyclopedia.* Ancient History Encyclopedia, 15 May 2015. Web. 23 Mar 2019.

[281] Woolf Greg, *Et Tu Brute? – The Murder of Caesar and Political Assassination.* 2006.

[282] Dierckx, Heidi M. C. *Greek and Roman Civilizations, Grade 5-8.* 2012.

[283] Ibid.

[284] History. "Cleopatra commits suicide." Web. Updated February 25, 2019.

but were unable to beat them. Cleopatra fled to Egypt and took refuge in her mausoleum.

Upon receiving the false message that Cleopatra was dead, Antony stabbed himself and was carried into her chamber where he found her alive.[285] Dying, he asked her to make peace with Octavius, but she did not. With no moves left to her, the Queen of Egypt killed herself. Octavius killed both Antony's oldest son, Antyllus, and the queen's son by Julius Caesar, Caesarion, and took Egypt for himself. In 27 BCE, he became Emperor Augustus of the Roman Empire, reigning for 41 years.[286] The three children born of Marc Antony and Cleopatra were sent to Antony's widow, Octavia, to be raised in Rome.[287]

---

[285] Ibid.

[286] Ibid.

[287] Haughton, Brian. "Cleopatra & Antony." *Ancient History Encyclopedia*. 10 Jan 2011. Web.

Chapter 21 – The City of Pompeii

Pompeii was one of the Roman Empire's largest cities, in which an estimated 20,000 people lived near the shore of the Bay of Naples under the shadow of Mount Vesuvius.[288] Formally settled in about the 8th century BCE, the Pompeii of 79 CE was a triumph of the Roman Empire.[289] The city was a bustling center for trade, likely selling olive oil, wine, and seafood to merchants from Rome, Spain, and Gaul.[290] Fortified by a stone wall, the city featured many luxuries of the day, including public baths, temples to Apollo and several other Greco-Roman gods, an immense amphitheater, and a public forum.[291] The citizens of this flourishing city participated in politics and trade, and they spent their free time watching the gladiatorial displays at the amphitheater. Wealthy and middle-class citizens alike owned slaves who took on a great deal of the

---

[288] Wilkinson, Paul. *Pompeii: An Archaeological Guide.* 2017.

[289] De Vos, Arnold and Mariette De Vos. *Pompeii, Herculaneum, Stabia.* 1982.

[290] Cartwright, Mark. "Trade in the Roman World." *Ancient History Encyclopedia.* 12 Apr 2018. Web. 24 Mar 2019.

[291] Berinato, Scott. "Crowd Control from Ancient Pompeii" *CSO.* Web. May 18, 2007.

agricultural work and food preparation, while the upper class took on the administrative duties of the community.

Though the people of the Roman Empire called the giant rock formation at the Bay of Naples a mountain, they were perfectly aware that it was actually a volcano. It had a long history dating back centuries as the source of small eruptions and earthquakes, and in 62 CE, there was a devastating earthquake that destroyed many buildings in Pompeii and nearby towns.[292] The damage had only been partially repaired by the year 79, after which point there would be no further opportunities to rebuild. That year, Mount Vesuvius exploded, covering the low-lying communities of Pompeii, Herculaneum, and smaller villages in thick layers of dust, ash, and pulverized rock.[293]

There had been warning signs for several days preceding the explosion in the form of earth tremors. These were not uncommon for the region, and so, there was not much precedent for alarm. By early afternoon, however, it was clear that this time, Vesuvius would not be calmed back into its centuries-long sleep.[294] A giant plume of ash, rock, and superheated air burst forth from the mouth of the mountain reaching 33 kilometers in height (21 miles).[295] In the precious few moments after the plume appeared above the mountain, citizens of all the surrounding villages and cities fled. Most of the inhabitants of Pompeii did make it out alive, probably on boats that took them from the shore of the city northward to the relative safety of Misenum.[296]

---

[292] Sintubin, M. *The Fires of Vesuvius.* 2010.

[293] Ibid.

[294] Ibid.

[295] Dobran, Flavio. *Vesuvius: Education, Security and Prosperity.* 2006.

[296] Wilkinson, Paul. *Pompeii: An Archaeological Guide.* 2017.

Misenum, which lay on the southern shore of part of the Italian landmass that jutted westward into the Mediterranean, was about 56 kilometers (35 miles) by land but considerably shorter by sea. It was mostly out of the way of the rain of pumice and ash that began falling down on Pompeii shortly after the plume first appeared, and thus, it stands to reason that many of the refugees fled in that direction. The people of Misenum weren't at all convinced that they were not in danger, however, and many of them fled farther north before the Pompeii escapees arrived.[297]

Among those who remained in Misenum was the writer Pliny the Younger, who looked out of his window in horror at the dark cloud growing over the city of Pompeii. His uncle, the esteemed Pliny the Elder, also saw the catastrophe unfolding and took it upon himself to get in a boat and document the event. Before he could leave, he was approached by a messenger who informed him that some of his friends were trapped at their house at the foot of the mountain. The terrified couple would only be able to evacuate via boat, so the elder Pliny agreed to go there immediately and try to help.[298]

He sailed directly toward the darkness across that small section of the sea and pushed through thick layers of rock and sediment that had built up along the opposite shore. On foot, he reached the home of his friends and was relieved to see that it was still mostly protected from the showers of ash. Pliny thought it best to assure his terrified friends that all was well and they would get through the storm safely, so he adopted a relaxed and confident attitude. Instead of fleeing back out into the hail of rocks, he was determined to wait out the worst of the eruption right where he was. He dined happily with his friends and even took a bath before falling asleep in a guest bedroom.[299]

---

[297] Pliny the Younger. *A Life in Roman Letters.*

[298] Ibid.

[299] Ibid.

Staying put turned out not to have been the best course of action since Pliny awoke in the middle of the night to find his room full of pumice and ash. He led the household, protected from falling rocks by pillows that they fastened to their heads, outside in search of their boats. However, escape via the water was impossible due to wild waves, so the group remained on shore, and Pliny collapsed onto the ground.[300]

Pliny the Younger wrote, "When daylight returned on the 26th—two days after the last day he had been seen—his body was found intact and uninjured, still fully clothed and looking more like sleep than death."

Pliny's friends seem to have made their escape and eventually told the tale to Pliny the Younger, as otherwise, the details of the journey would have fallen victim to history along with Pliny the Elder. Unfortunately for the younger writer and natural historian, he would never again see his uncle, namesake, and mentor. Though it is often supposed that the would-be rescuer died from inhaling toxic fumes from the volcano, it seems more likely that he first suffered an asthmatic attack and then succumbed to suffocation from ash or a heart attack. The nephew documented the fact that his uncle was in possession of a weak windpipe, and therefore, some physical ailment connected with the thickening air and fear of the moment probably were to blame for the elder Pliny's death.

Even then, the catastrophe wasn't over. The cloud of rock and ash poured out from Vesuvius for two days, and by the early morning of the second day, pyroclastic flows rocketed down the sides of the mountain and straight through the walls of Pompeii and nearby Herculaneum.[301] Any people still trapped in the cities, battling falling rocks on their way out or hiding under solid roofs, were quickly killed in the fast-moving wave of hot gas and rock. In all, an

---

[300] Ibid.

[301] Wilkinson, Paul. *Pompeii: An Archaeological Guide.* 2017.

estimated 1500 people died in and around Pompeii during those two days of horror, and though most citizens did manage to flee in time to save themselves, there was nothing for them to come back to.[302] The walls, temples, bathhouses, public areas, and homes were all buried under up to 7 meters (23 feet) of ash and volcanic rock.[303] Some of the refugees returned home once the ash ceased to fall, but they found nothing to salvage and no one left visible, let alone alive. Little by little, the citizens gave up on their home and retreated farther inland, away from the cause of their devastation.

Mount Vesuvius showed no remorse, spreading its choking darkness over cities and communities for miles around for days after it went silent. In Misenum, Pliny the Younger was grief-stricken at the loss of his uncle and shocked at the magnitude of the tragedy. In a letter to his friend and historian, Cornelius Tacitus, he described the chaos of the evacuation that took place in his relatively distant city:

> Though my shocked soul recoils, my tongue shall tell. Though it was now morning, the light was still exceedingly faint and doubtful; the buildings all around us tottered, and though we stood upon open ground, yet as the place was narrow and confined, there was no remaining without imminent danger: we therefore resolved to quit the town. A panic-stricken crowd followed us, and (as to a mind distracted with terror every suggestion seems more prudent than its own) pressed on us in dense array to drive us forward as we came out. Being at a convenient distance from the houses, we stood still, in the midst of a most dangerous and dreadful scene.
>
> The chariots, which we had ordered to be drawn out, were so agitated backwards and forwards, though upon the most level ground, that we could not keep them steady, even by

---

[302] Moormann, Eric. *Pompeii's Ashes*. 2015.

[303] Sutton, Mark Q. *Achaeology: The Science of the Human Past*. 2015.

supporting them with large stones. The sea seemed to roll back upon itself, and to be driven from its banks by the convulsive motion of the earth; it is certain at least the shore was considerably enlarged, and several sea animals were left upon it. On the other side, a black and dreadful cloud, broken with rapid, zigzag flashes, revealed behind it variously shaped masses of flame: these last were like sheet-lightning, but much larger.

The buried remains of Italy's sparkling coastal city stayed hidden for nearly 1,700 years, long after the Romans had once more clustered together under the shadow of the great mountain.[304]

[304] Kleiner, Fred S. *Gardner's Art Through the Ages.* 2009.

Chapter 22 – Antonine and Cyprian Plagues

Not even Vesuvius could stop the Roman war machine. In the years following the great tragedy at Pompeii, the empire's soldiers continued their steady march into Europe and Asia by the tens of thousands. Though a significant amount of trade was lost due to the disappearance of Pompeii's great industries of wool-spinning, cloth-dying, oil-pressing, and fish paste production, the economy did not drag for long.[305] Money never wavered when it came to the military; the army would press onward no matter what the emperor had to do to make it so.

Rome's armies were populated by a mixture of natural-born Romans and people who had been naturalized into Roman citizens from the many kingdoms and provinces under the control of the empire.[306] All of them served on long missions away from home for many years, from a standard two decades to as many as four decades. At the end of a long campaign, soldiers who were not needed for administration or defense flooded back to Rome to rest and await their next

---

[305] HSC Resources. "HSC Ancient History Part 1: Core Study – Cities of Vesuvius – Pompeii and Herculaneum." *Dux College.* Web.
[306] Breeze, David J. *The Roman Army.* 2016.

assignment. Those who'd finished their contracts came home for good.

In 165 CE, a particularly large influx of soldiers returning to Italy from their campaigns in western Asia brought back more than their part of the spoils of war: they brought a nasty virus too.[307] The sickness was first scientifically observed by the Greek physician Galen during his stay in Aquileia, located in northern Italy, in the winter of 168 CE.[308] He'd been bidden to come to Rome by co-emperors Marcus Aurelius and Lucius Verus, as they were desperate for his help and input on the matter of the disease that had been rampant already for three years. Galen described the outbreak of that same sickness in Aquileia as being characterized by a fever, sore throat, and diarrhea.[309] He also noted that on the ninth day of illness, sufferers' skins broke out in pustular and dry sores.

The disease spread, following the route of the empire's soldiers home and then radiating out from Italy into the cities and provinces of the north. It is said to have wiped out entire communities and so badly crippled the Roman army that further expansion of the empire was put on hold; Marcus Aurelius himself joined his troops at the German front to oversee the constant pushback of the Germanic tribes along Rome's frontier border.[310] Fortunately for the emperor's dwindling ranks, the Germans' own people were also under attack from the deadly virus.

The wheels of the great engine that was the Roman Empire continued to turn, plague or not, and its diplomats were spread from Britannia to China. A political meetup between a representative of

---

[307] Cunningham, Kevin. *The Bubonic Plague.* 2011.

[308] Kohn, Samuel Kline. *Epidemics: Hate and Compassion.* 2018.

[309] Ibid.

[310] Sabbatani, S. and S. Fiorino. "The Antonine Plague and the decline of the Roman Empire." *US National Library of Medicine, National Institutes of Health.* 17 December 2009.

Aurelius and the Han court of Emperor Huan in 166 CE matches up with the first plague year which was suffered by both empires.[311] The visit was meant to facilitate trade agreements between the realms, which would have been an enormous boon for Rome's elite. Instead of ushering in a new age of intercontinental commerce based on silk, tea, and porcelain from the Far East and gold, silver, wool, and steel from the west, sickness and death crept in, massively slowing the advancement of both civilizations and seriously postponing any such enhanced trade between the two.

For Rome, extended and widespread sickness meant losing out on money and goods that had been coming from the Indian Ocean. Like the emperor out on the front lines of battle, holding back the encroaching tribes, the empire itself ground its gears and merely held its own for at least several decades. The realm began to recover in the first quarter of the 3rd century CE when Roman Emperor Septimius Severus invaded the lands north of Hadrian's Wall.[312] The invasion of what Severus called Caledonia went well at first, but it turned sour when Severus died less than three years later, and eventually, the land was once more relinquished to the natives.[313]

The spirit of the empire was in jeopardy at that point, and in 238 CE, Rome suffered an unprecedented crisis of political faith. It would be called the Year of the Six Emperors, thanks to a split between the Senate-approved co-emperors Gordian I and Gordian II, and the military-elected Emperor Maximus Thrax.[314] They clashed at the Battle of Carthage that same year, and Maximus' forces killed Gordian II. Gordian I killed himself, leaving the empire in the hands

---

[311] Pulleyblank, Edwin G. "The Roman Empire as Known to Han China", *Journal of the American Oriental Society.* Vol. 119, No. 1. 1999.

[312] Merrony, Mark. *The Plight of Rome in the Fifth Century AD.* 2017.

[313] Birley, Anthony R. *Septimius Severus: The African Emperor.* 1999.

[314] Newton, Michael. *Famous Assassinations in World History.* 2014.

of Maximus. Not to be dismissed, the Senate elected two more co-emperors: Pupienus and Balbinus.[315]

The Senate's decision was not a popular one; though the citizens of Rome would not accept Maximus as their ruler, neither did they accept the rapidly elected replacements of the Gordians. To appease the people, the Senate offered 13-year-old Gordian III, heir to his deceased namesakes, the title of Caesar.[316] The other three so-called emperors were murdered by competing factions of the army, leaving only young Gordian in power for the next six years. He, too, died in battle, and the quick successions continued while a second plague struck the capital city and empire.

This second illness hit around the year 249 CE and didn't abate for over twenty years.[317] Crippled once more, Rome truly struggled to right itself this time around. It lacked clear leadership, faced plummeting numbers in the army and at home tending the farms, and there was intense warfare at the northern and eastern borders of the realm. Rome constantly battled against the Goths in Germany and the Sasanian Empire of Persia, losing ground on both fronts. Again, the sickness shook the already unsteady Roman Empire to its core.

Medical historians believe the illness that covered most of the northern hemisphere during both plague periods was smallpox, though measles and other types of viruses have also been posited.[318] The massive loss of life suffered in Rome and throughout the Roman Empire during the Antonine and Cyprian Plagues very seriously affected the civilizations of all Europe, Asia, and North Africa. The Romans nearly did not recover in the midst of such sickness, death, and political instability, but by 285 CE, the empire finally had a

---

[315] Ibid.

[316] Ibid.

[317] Harper, Kyle. *The Fate of Rome*. 2017.

[318] Bollyky, Thomas J. *Plagues and the Paradox of Progress*. 2018.

more long-lasting ruler with Emperor Maximus.[319] Once more, the Roman Empire had achieved enough balance to move forward into the future.

---

[319] Wasson, Donald L. "Diocletian." *Ancient History Encyclopedia.*Web. 2 Feb 2014.

Chapter 23 – Britannia and Londinium

It is possible that the city of London was initially named for ravens or a raven-deity. But the word closely resembles "Lugdunum," the Roman name for both the city of Lyon in France and Leiden in the Netherlands. That Roman name, in turn, was derived from the Celtic "Lugdon," which meant, literally, "hill, or town, of the god Lugh" or, alternatively, "...of ravens." Whether or not "Lugdunum" was the origin of "London," ravens were important for inhabitants of Britain for both practical and religious reasons.

(Boria Sax, *City of Ravens*)

At the far northwestern reaches of the great Roman Empire lay two isolated islands just off mainland Europe. Home to various tribes of Iron Age peoples, including the Celts, the islands were considered barbaric, cold, and uncomfortable for Roman nobility and soldiers alike.[320] Nevertheless, Emperor Claudius desired to leave no lands—no matter how roughly hewn—untouched by the hand of his vast empire. In the year 43 CE, Claudius marched his legions forth to cross over the sea and march through the wilderness of the ancient

---

[320] Chappell, Gavin. *Celtic Dawn*. 2003.

British Isles.[321] The first and largest of these he meant to conquer; the second, modern Ireland, was left mostly to its own devices.

Roman armies were experts in world domination, having already annexed up to 70 million citizens of Europe, North Africa, and western Asia.[322] They knew how to march into new lands, fight in organized units, and force local warriors and kings to bend the knee. Once that had been accomplished, they set their brute strength to building camps, infrastructure, and, eventually, new cities in the Roman style.

Emperors believed that every urban center ruled by civilized Rome should have a central forum that served as a public gathering place, business district, and marketplace; this was surrounded by rectangular blocks of homes, shops, and other public buildings.[323] Two diagonal main streets crossed perpendicularly over the forum, and a protective wall surrounded the city. It was a blueprint for city-building that the empire's builders, laborers, and architects—most of whom were already employed within the vast army—used time and time again.

On the northern bank of the river Thames, in what the Romans called Britannia, this very same method was employed.[324] It began with a bridge over the river and an army camp, but it would become much, much more. The process of city-building in the wild lands of Britannia was not easy; Romans had difficulty making allies among the various local tribes and suffered a multitude of uprisings, like that of Queen Boudica of the Iceni in about 60 CE.[325] Overwhelmed by the revolt, the city was abandoned by the Romans until the

---

[321] Gagarin, Michael. *The Oxford Encyclopedia of Ancient Greece and Rome.* 2009.

[322] Campbell, Kenneth L. *Western Civilization.* 2014.

[323] Morris, Anthony E. *History of Urban Form: Prehistory to the Renaissance.* 1972.

[324] Fraser, Rebecca. *The Story of Britain: From the Romans to the Present.* 2006.

[325] Mark, Joshua J. "Boudicca." *Ancient History Encyclopedia.* Web. 8 November 2013.

uprising could be stopped. By the time the heavily outnumbered Roman forces stopped the attacks, the new city had been destroyed. Roman documents suggest that as many as 70,000 people died during the revolt, with several cities burning into ashes at the torch of the rebellious queen.[326]

It was nothing the Roman Empire and its generals hadn't seen before, however; the city was rebuilt soon afterward and in another short half-century had grown to become the bustling city of Londinium, home to as many as 60,000 Romans and Britons.[327] It was the pride of Roman Britannia. Multitudes of paved roads were constructed between Londinium and dozens of other Romanized towns and cities across the southern half of the island, reaching an estimated 3,200 kilometers (2,000 miles) in total distance.[328] Like a wildly successful virus, Rome reached its tendrils across the land and formed masses of communities and military forts.

Londinium prospered for several reasons, the first of which was its location along southern Britannia's most important waterway. Along the Thames, one could easily transport soldiers, food, building equipment, and other supplies within the city to outlying towns. The second reason for its success was the relatively mild climate, which soldiers were able to tolerate much better than the cold reaches of the island's far north. In effect, the city was suitably comfortable and well supplied with resources of trout, deer, rabbits, herbs, root vegetables, leafy greens, apples, and other foodstuffs. If the conquering civilization could manage to keep the local cultures suppressed, Rome could potentially protect its British claim for centuries from the fortified city of Londinium.

---

[326] Frenee-Hutchins, Samantha. *Boudica's Odyssey in Early Modern England.* 2016.

[327] Rollason, Jane. *London Level 2 Elementary.* 2014.

[328] Sell, Peter J. *Women the Power Behind the Crown of England.* 2017.

Emperor Hadrian took it upon himself to travel thousands of kilometers from his seat of power in Italy to Britannia in 122 CE.[329] Upon reaching the farthest part of his empire, Hadrian ordered his garrisons to build a wall across the northern border of Britannia to protect the Roman realm from northern tribes. The project commenced immediately and reached 117 kilometers (73 miles) east to west.[330] Personal and administrative wooden tablets, used for long-distance communication before the use of paper became widespread, are littered around the wall's ancient Fort Vindolanda and other sites along the wall.[331] These tablets have served to catalog some of the intimate details of Rome's northernmost outpost in Britannia. Lists of inventories and requests for supplies include food and a great deal of wooden pieces, from cart axles to planks, for a bed.[332] It is clear that they thirsted for the food, drink, and luxuries of home, but thanks to a well-maintained network of roads and internal routes from one end of the empire to the other, it was entirely possible to bring sweet chestnuts from Spain all the way to Hadrian's Wall.[333]

Within a decade of Emperor Hadrian's visit to Britannia, a fire destroyed a great deal of Londinium.[334] Known as the Hadrianic Fire, it was nearly as destructive as the forces of Queen Boudica had been in the previous century. Persistent, the empire rebuilt the pride of its most northern province, sending food, building supplies, human resources, and gold and silver coins minted in Rome itself.

[329] Kreitzer, Larry Joseph. *Striking New Images.* 1996.

[330] Fagan, Dr. Brian and Chris Scarre. *Ancient Civilizations.* 2015.

[331] Daley, Jason. "Cache of Roman Messages Found Near Hadrian's Wall." *Smithsonian.* Web. 11 July 2017.

[332] Vindolanda Tablets Online.

[333] Ibid.

[334] Milford, Anna. *London in Flames.* 1998.

Hadrian's empire was at its peak, and there was virtually nothing he couldn't accomplish at the hand of his army, which was responsible for infrastructure maintenance as well as military might and defense. During his reign, he showered Britannia with the funds necessary to build, rebuild, and permanently imprint the Roman culture upon the face of this distant island. Indeed, the cult of the Romans clung fiercely to Britain long after the empire itself had faded away.

Chapter 24 – Remnants of Classical Antiquity

Like the generations of leaves, the lives of mortal men. Now the wind scatters the old leaves across the earth, now the living timber bursts with the new buds and spring comes round again. And so with men: as one generation comes to life, another dies away.

(Homer, the *Iliad*)

In 1748, the city of Pompeii was rediscovered, frozen in time, by an excavation team commissioned by the King of Naples, Charles of Bourbon.[335] Ironically, the necropolis of the lost city was one of the first pieces of Pompeii to be uncovered. It was a shocking link to the ancient ancestors of modern Italians.

The decline of the old empire was gradual, punctuated by the adoption of Christianity as its official religion in the 4th century.[336] By that point, the work of Greco-Roman scientists and philosophers

---

[335] Foss, Pedar, and John J. Dobbins (editors.) *The World of Pompeii.* 2009.

[336] Novak, Ralph Martin. *Christianity and the Roman Empire.* 2001.

had done the work of eradicating ancient pantheons from the contemporary mindset; the encroachment of Christianity in the early centuries of the new millennium proved an adequate replacement for Rome's lost spirituality. Apollo, Gaia, Jupiter, and their brethren were replaced by Jesus Christ and the Christian-Judaic monotheism.

The period of Late Antiquity was characterized by the movement of Christianity through Europe. Rome's influence waned by degrees in the 3rd and 4th centuries, and in the farthest northern reaches of the empire, continued attacks from the Picts proved unsustainable for Roman settlements. Soldiers, statesmen, governors, and settlers flooded out of Britannia over the next century as Anglo-Saxons from western Europe increased immigration to the island. The same occurred in Brittany and most of western Europe thanks to the repeated pressure of Germanic armies, resulting in a period of minimal education, political chaos, and regional violence known as the Dark Ages.

The eastern region of the Roman Empire eventually split from the west, forming the Byzantine Empire. The western section consolidated portions of itself into the Holy Roman Empire in the 8th century and actually maintained a great deal of its former influence, if not landmass.[337] Very much in keeping with its historical style, the Holy Roman Empire rebranded itself as the center of religious knowledge and worship for all Christendom. They built an entire city within Rome for the leader of the Catholic Church, which became the driving force behind the politics and wars of the Middle Ages. The Holy Roman Empire lasted until 1806 when it was annexed by Napoleon of France.[338] The Catholic Pope's home, the independent city-state named Vatican City, remains within Rome to this day.

---

[337] Heer, Friedrich. *The Holy Roman Empire.* 2002.

[338] Encyclopædia Britannica. "Holy Roman Empire." Web.

The pieces of the Greek and Roman Empires can still be found now, scattered from London to Babylon. The 2nd-century Pantheon of Rome still stands, having been regularly maintained and put to use since it was first constructed. Today, it serves as a Catholic church. The Amphitheatre of Pompeii is the oldest of its kind still standing in Italy today, though it had to be dug out of the debris from Mount Vesuvius before it could be added to the archaeological record.[339] It took many decades of sporadic searching and digging to unearth a significant portion of the ash-buried community of Pompeii, but much of that work was undertaken by Italian archaeologist Giuseppe Fiorelli and his team.

Fiorelli realized that the people of Pompeii could be preserved alongside their beautiful city thanks to a simple mixture of plaster.[340] The bodies of those killed by falling debris and the pyroclastic flows from Mount Vesuvius in 79 CE had decomposed within their burial mound, leaving behind a person-shaped void in the layers of rock. By pouring plaster carefully into those voids, archaeologists were able to recreate the people who had been buried—complete with skeletons and teeth. By removing the rock and hardened ash layers around the plaster, whole humans emerged out of time.[341] They can be visited at the site of the old city which is now a World Heritage Site. In 1891, a brand-new Pompei sprang forth on the outskirts of the old thanks to a series of miracles reported at the Shrine of the Virgin of the Rosary of Pompeii.[342]

Even where the physical remains are few, Greek and Roman culture still abound in the forms of electoral processes, city administration, stonemasonry, concrete construction, libraries, schools, government houses, literature, and even theater. The Greek tragedies and

---

[339] Berry, Dr. Joanne. "Pompeii Art and Architecture Gallery." *BBC*. Web. 2011.

[340] Archaeology. "Casts of Pompeii." Web.

[341] Ibid.

[342] Longo, Bartolo. *History of the Sanctuary of Pompeii*. 1895.

Homer's poetry remain within the foundations of educational literature, and the Socratic method is the premise upon which all Western philosophic pursuits are based. Mathematics, astronomy, and political sciences of the Western world would be vacuous if one removed all that was once Greek or Roman.

In essence, intellectual philosophy is the keystone to the great Greco-Roman civilization. Without it, there would be little of note to write about this culture except that, like those before and after, it conquered, grew large, and eventually shrank. Philosophy, fortunately, established itself firmly in Athens and Rome and provided the great thinkers of the Classical period the means by which to examine themselves and the world around them. They left these gifts of perspective, self-analysis, and natural wonder to those of us who tread the earth in their stead.

Check out more books by Captivating History

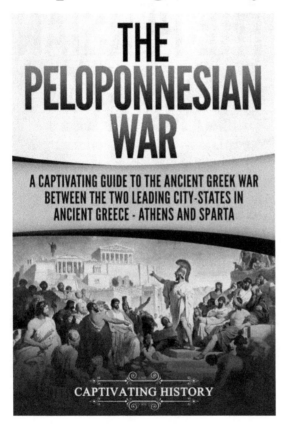

THE
PELOPONNESIAN
WAR

A CAPTIVATING GUIDE TO THE ANCIENT GREEK WAR
BETWEEN THE TWO LEADING CITY-STATES IN
ANCIENT GREECE - ATHENS AND SPARTA

CAPTIVATING HISTORY

THE PERSIAN EMPIRE

A CAPTIVATING GUIDE TO THE HISTORY OF PERSIA, STARTING FROM THE ANCIENT ACHAEMENID, PARTHIAN, AND SASSANIAN EMPIRES TO THE SAFAVID, AFSHARID, AND QAJAR DYNASTIES

CAPTIVATING HISTORY

SPARTANS

A CAPTIVATING GUIDE TO THE FIERCE WARRIORS OF
ANCIENT GREECE, INCLUDING SPARTAN MILITARY TACTICS, THE
BATTLE OF THERMOPYLAE, HOW SPARTA WAS RULED AND MORE

CAPTIVATING HISTORY

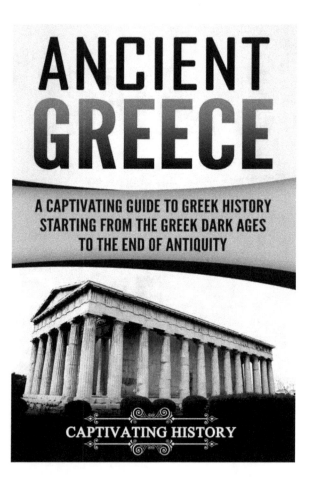

ANCIENT GREECE

A CAPTIVATING GUIDE TO GREEK HISTORY STARTING FROM THE GREEK DARK AGES TO THE END OF ANTIQUITY

CAPTIVATING HISTORY

Free Bonus from Captivating History (Available for a Limited time)

Hi History Lovers!

Now you have a chance to join our exclusive history list so you can get your first history ebook for free as well as discounts and a potential to get more history books for free! Simply visit the link below to join.

Captivatinghistory.com/ebook

Also, make sure to follow us on Facebook, Twitter and Youtube by searching for Captivating History.

CPSIA information can be obtained
at www.ICGtesting.com
Printed in the USA
LVHW082252290422
717543LV00003B/129